Unlocked

CHESHIRE PRIZE FOR LITERATURE ANTHOLOGIES

Prize Flights: Stories from the Cheshire Prize for Literature 2003; edited by **Ashley Chantler**

Life Lines: Poems from the Cheshire Prize for Literature 2004; edited by **Ashley Chantler**

Word Weaving: Stories and Poems for Children from the Cheshire Prize for Literature 2005; edited by **Jaki Brien**

Edge Words: Stories from the Cheshire Prize for Literature 2006; edited by **Peter Blair**

Elements: Poems from the Cheshire Prize for Literature 2007; edited by **Peter Blair**

Wordscapes: Stories and Poems for Children from the Cheshire Prize for Literature 2008; edited by **Jaki Brien**

Zoo: Short Stories from the Cheshire Prize for Literature 2009; edited by **Emma L. E. Rees**

Still Life: Poetry from the Cheshire Prize for Literature 2010; edited by **Emma L. E. Rees**

Wordlife: Stories and Poems for Children from the Cheshire Prize for Literature 2011; edited by **Jaki Brien**

Lost and Found: Short Stories from the Cheshire Prize for Literature 2012; edited by **Emma L. E. Rees**

Great Escapes: Poetry from the Cheshire Prize for Literature 2013; edited by **Emma L. E. Rees**

Out of this Word: Stories and Poems for Children from the Cheshire Prize for Literature 2014; edited by **Jaki Brien**

Patches of Light: Short Stories from the Cheshire Prize for Literature 2015; edited by **Ian Seed**

Crossings Over: Poetry from the Cheshire Prize for Literature 2016; edited by **Ian Seed**

Opening Words: Stories and Poems for Children from the Cheshire Prize for Literature 2017; edited by **Simon E. Poole**

Island Chain: Short Stories from the Cheshire Prize for Literature 2018; edited by **William Stephenson**

Unlocked

Writing from the
Cheshire Prize for Literature 2020

Edited by
Simon E. Poole
and
William Stephenson

University of Chester Press

First published 2021
by the University of Chester Press
Parkgate Road
Chester CH1 4BJ

Printed and bound in the UK by the
LIS Print Unit
University of Chester

Cover designed by the LIS Graphics Team
University of Chester

This collection © University of Chester, 2021
Individual contributions © their respective authors

The right of Simon E. Poole and William Stephenson to be identified as the joint editors of this work have been asserted in accordance with the Copyright, Designs and Patents Act 1988

The moral rights of the contributors to be identified as the authors of this work have been asserted in accordance with the Copyright, Designs and Patents Act 1988

All Rights Reserved
No part of this publication may be reproduced, stored in a retrieval system or transmitted in any form or by any means without the prior permission of the copyright owner, other than as permitted by UK copyright legislation or under the terms and conditions of a recognised copyright licensing scheme

A catalogue record of this book is available from the British Library

ISBN 978-1-910481-10-3

CONTENTS

Contributors	viii
Foreword	xvi
A Rock Called Pluto *Leon Coleman*	1
Relative Humidity *Esther Amis-Hughes*	4
One Fossil to Another *Sheila Tyrer Hughes*	9
The Craft *Jennifer Grey*	13
The Really Good Book Club Papers *Rebecca Kershaw*	17
Leaving Room for God's Wrath *Nicola Russell Johnson*	22
Still Life *Matthew Rushton*	26
New Backgrounds *Chris Nelson*	29
Lockdown 2041 *Janys Chambers*	34
Freddie the Field Mouse *Carol Howard*	39

Unlocked

George and the Number Thirty-Eight Bus — 43
Joy Bryce

Ben's (Boring) Lockdown Journal — 48
Yvonne Oliver-Redfern

Home-Schooling Hero — 54
Sheila Blackburn

Granny Finola has a Scream — 57
Angi Holden

Residue — 61
Paul Howarth

Three Lockdown Days — 63
Jane Thomas

Home Alone — 65
Dick Gilpin

Christmas Tree Worms — 67
Helen Kay

Northwich — 68
Kemal Houghton

An Intangible Loss — 70
Chris Hollis-Thompson

Embracing a New Normal — 73
Joanne Stokes

Shortness of Breath — 75
Matthew Byrne

During Lockdown — 77
Morgan McIntyre

Contents

Delamere Forest *George Alldred*	78
Dear Strangers *Dana Roberts*	80
Remember That Time? *Zoë Lambrakis*	82
Home Sweet Home *Caitlin Norbury*	84
I Am Stars *Julie McKiernan*	100
Game Time *Roberto Rodriguez*	109
Small Talk *Tim Elgood*	124
Rose Walker *Simon James*	137
Your Courage, Your Cheerfulness, Your Resolution Will Bring Us Victory *Ben Saunders*	155

CONTRIBUTORS

George Alldred is a recent university graduate, who now works as an accountant in Manchester. Poetry does not fall naturally within the bounds of his day-to-day life and this was his first ever competitive entry. When writing, he often draws inspiration from the nature around him and its metaphorical edge, very much in the style of Pablo Neruda. The frost on that cold winter's day truly allowed him to express his frustration at the isolation and stagnation of lockdown.

Esther Amis-Hughes was born in Macclesfield, but went to university in Leeds, and never left Yorkshire. To her children's irritation she still often (accidentally) refers to Cheshire as home. She writes short fiction, in recent years the shorter the better, mostly because she has to write whilst waiting for under-ten football training to finish. Flash fiction is the perfect medium for this mum/taxi-driver.

Sheila Blackburn has enjoyed forty years as a Cheshire primary school teacher and loves writing stories, poems and books for children. Lockdown provided very different experiences and the chance to find ways to smile about the challenges faced by all of us, especially families required to take on home schooling ... it also provided some interesting writing material. Irresistible ... !

Joy Bryce grew up on the Wirral and gained a degree in English Literature and Education at undergraduate level. She taught English in this country and in Italy for several years before qualifying as a primary school teacher. Her interest in writing for children stems from her own love of books and work. The Cheshire Prize is her first experience of competition. She lives in Cheshire.

Contributors

Matthew Byrne can be found taking in the sights and sounds beside Cheshire's majestic River Gowy, gaining inspiration for his art from nature's abundance alongside the riverbank.

Janys Chambers is a freelance playwright and director who lives in North Wales but has worked extensively in Cheshire. She has previously received nominations for Best Production for Children in the Manchester Theatre Awards; Best Episode in a Soap in the TV Soap Awards; and Best Radio Play for Children with The Writers Guild. She has been BAFTA Nominated Best New Writer to Television and won a shared BAFTA Cymru for Best Series. She has never entered a short story into a competition before.

Leon Coleman's fiction has appeared in literary magazines, including *Litro Online* (November 2021), *The Fiction Pool, Bandit, Literally Stories, Misery Tourism* and elsewhere. In 2019, he won third prize in the Henshaw Press Short Story Competition. In the same year, he was longlisted in the University of Sunderland Short Story in Association with Waterstones Award. He is currently working on his short story collection.

Tim Elgood worked as a social worker in Cheshire way back in the 1970s and is still in contact with some of the "children in care" (now in their fifties) he helped to support. He commenced writing for youth and community theatre groups and has subsequently had plays professionally produced at both the Derby Playhouse and Chesterfield Pomegranate Theatre. With the onset of Covid restrictions Tim has focussed upon short plays for radio.

Unlocked

Dick Gilpin lives now in retirement in the south of Cheshire, which is almost Shropshire and very nearly Wales. Work has mostly been in the North West apart from three years working in the then West Berlin – an island surrounded by East Germany. Poetry, being quite different from work projects, has been the chance to think with words and spaces, exploring the depths of our daily experiences.

Jennifer Gray, who is originally from rural Aberdeenshire, studied English with Creative Writing at the University of Chester. Her first novel was shortlisted for the Mslexia Women's Novel Competition. Her poetry and short fiction have appeared in publications such as *Neon*, *Flash* and *Glasgow Women Poets*. Jennifer holds an MSc in Creative Writing from the University of Edinburgh and currently lives in Dublin.

Angi Holden is a retired lecturer, whose published work includes poetry, short stories and flash fictions. She won the Victoria Baths Splash Fiction competition, and the Mother's Milk Poetry Prize for her pamphlet *Spools of Thread*. Her short story "Preserving History" was selected for Open Book New Writing 2021.

Chris Hollis-Thompson, who has been a Cheshire resident for most of his life to date, resides in Chester. He is self-published under his pen name Hollis Thompson and has featured in a previous Cheshire Prize for Literature anthology.

Kemal Houghton lives in Bebington. He is Chair of Chester Poets, a co-presenter at First Thursday in Heswall and is on the planning group for the Wirral Poetry Festival. His work has appeared in Chester Poets' Anthologies since 1981 and various magazines in print and online. His pamphlet, *There Will Be Dancing* came out with Red Squirrel Press in 2020.

Contributors

Carol Howard is a preschool French tutor, teaching in Cheshire and further afield. Inspired by the children she works with, she enjoys writing short stories in rhyme. Over the last few years her work has been featured on the Scholastic Resource Bank. Carol is an active member of St Helens Writers' Club.

Paul Howarth was born in Chester. Having spent much of his life in Cheshire, he now lives and works near the Suffolk coast. He has work published in various magazines and anthologies, including *We've Done Nothing Wrong. We've Nothing to Hide* (Verve), *Eighty Four: Poems on Male Suicide* (Verve) and *The Result is What You See Today* (Smith|Doorstop).

Simon James lived in Cheshire for the first eighteen years of his life before moving to Lancaster University, where he received a first-class degree in English and Creative Writing. After graduating, Simon wrote a short play which starred Jude Law, a comic book which has had its adaptation rights bought by Netflix, and over thirty episodes of clip shows on channels such as Comedy Central and Channel 5. "Rose Walker" was inspired by Simon's experience of working from home over lockdown alongside his partner Hannah, who is a primary school teacher in Chester.

Helen Kay is a Dabber born and bred. Her work has appeared in various magazines. She was highly commended in the 2020 Welsh Poetry Awards. She curates a project to support dyslexic poets: dyslexiapoetry.co.uk. Her pamphlet, *This Lexia & Other Languages* (V. Press) was published in 2020. She is known on Facebook for her sidekick hen puppet, Nigella.

Unlocked

Rebecca Kershaw was at college in Chester then went on to gain an MA in Creative Writing at Sheffield Hallam. She has won short story competitions, including the Fathom Prize and had her stories published in magazines. She now lives in the countryside, from which she draws inspiration for her writing and where she grows flowers and vegetables.

Zoë Lambrakis is a British Greek actress/writer from Chester. Having graduated from Warwick University with a BA in Theatre and Performance Studies, she went on to study acting at the Oxford School of Drama and has been working in London theatre since 2014. Although a writer of poetry since school, the Cheshire Prize is the first competition that she has entered.

Morgan McIntyre graduated with a BA in English and Creative Writing with First Class Honours. She has lived in Merseyside, Cumbria, Cheshire, Devon and China, and enjoys drawing upon these experiences in her poetry and fiction. She recently wrote the winning Fiction Category entry in the Plymouth University 2021 edition of *INK*.

Julie McKiernan studied Drama and Creative Writing at Crewe & Alsager College then taught adults with learning disabilities at Gorse Covert in Cheshire. After twenty-five years of teaching teenagers she became a feral writer specialising in heritage scripts and life stories and supplementing her income by teaching writing in Runcorn.

Chris Nelson is an author, designer and illustrator. He lives in the UK near the sea. His work tends to explore his increasingly distrustful relationship with technology. He hopes to one day save the world and own a pinball machine.

Contributors

Caitlin Norbury was born in Manchester and now lives in Cheshire. She recently gained a Screenwriting Master's from the University of Manchester and hopes to work in the film and TV industry in the future.

Yvonne Oliver-Redfern was born and grew up on the Wirral. She has a degree in Drama and English and enjoys writing in her spare time. Her work has featured in previous Cheshire Prize for Literature publications in both the adult and children's writing categories, as well as in Reflex Fiction publications.

Dana Roberts grew up in Chester and attended the University of Leeds where she studied Psychology. She has enjoyed writing from a young age, and her other hobbies include art, music, travel and volunteering.

Roberto Rodriguez has a BA in English Literature and an MA in American Literature from the University of Leeds. He has worked as a journalist and literary consultant. He was the winner of the Ted Walters Poetry Competition for his poem "The See-Saw", which was also published by *The Interpreter's House* magazine.

Matthew Rushton taught English in Cheshire for several years. He lives in Manchester and when he is not trying to get young people to read short stories, he attempts to write them himself.

Unlocked

Nicola Russell Johnson lives in Cheshire with her other half, two kids and ducks. She spent four years travelling and teaching before settling down to get a PhD in Creative Writing and work as a ghost writer. Since having children she's become about as sentient as room temperature yoghurt, however with the youngest starting school soon, she's starting to pick up the pen and has already won a couple of rounds of the NYC Midnight contest. Plus, she's over the moon to be shortlisted here again. She is hoping this year to reclaim her creative brain cells, and encourage them to start writing again, instead of just singing "Baby Shark" over and over and over – doo doo do, do do doo.

Ben Saunders writes plays and stories which intertwine everyday characters with out of the ordinary situations. He studied Natural Sciences and Psychology at Durham University, before gaining a PhD in the Psychology of Discourse from the University of Manchester. He lived in Cheshire before moving to Manchester where he currently lives with his family. His first novel, *Senescence: The Ashes of Youth* is now available on Amazon, before its wider book store release.

Joanne Stokes is Yorkshire born and bred but has lived in Chester for over four years now, following her career in jewellery retail, then starting a young family with baby number two on the way. Creative writing is a talent which stems in the family and is something Joanne discovered she enjoyed at school. By no means a professional thing, it is more a hobby and Joanne writes in the moment during her spare time.

Jane Thomas grew up on the Wirral and went to West Kirby Grammar; she also established Port Sunlight Poets while living in the village. She is now based in Oxford and has recently been shortlisted in *The Rialto* Open Pamphlet Competition, The Poetry Society's Stanza Poetry Competition and The FPM-Hippocrates Prize and published in: *Stand, The Rialto, Envoi, Mslexia* and the *ORB*. She is currently completing a collection focussed on Alzheimer's.

Contributors

Sheila Tyrer Hughes's love of writing began at school alongside her love of reading. It became a serious pastime in the late sixties when she was living in California taking care of children and horses. On her return to Wales she went to training college and continued writing while teaching and bringing up two boys. In 2005 she was joint runner-up in the Cheshire Prize and in 2007 she read a prize-winning story at the Barbican. This will be the seventh Cheshire anthology in which her work has appeared. In 2016 she achieved a long-held ambition and now has two children's books in print. A third book is due out soon and a fourth currently in production.

Si Poole (editor) is an Associate Professor of Cultural Education at the University of Chester, Programme Leader for the MA Creative Practices in Education and Senior Lead in Cultural Education and Research at Storyhouse; Trustee of the Mythstories Museum of Myth and Fable; Researcher at the Centre for Research in Education, Creativity and Arts through Practice and the International Thriving at Work Centre. Poet, songwriter and singer with The Loose Kites.

William Stephenson (editor) is an Associate Professor of Modern and Contemporary Literature at the University of Chester. He has published numerous research articles and three academic books. His poetry collection *Travellers and Avatars* (Live Canon, 2018) was shortlisted for the Live Canon First Collection Prize. His second collection *The Lotus Bunker* is forthcoming from Live Canon.

FOREWORD

William and I have chatted about how best to present this year's shortlisted entries for the Cheshire Prize for Literature in a way that befits the unusual circumstances in which they've been written. We also wanted to highlight the unusual approach we took to the prize this year in response to lockdown. We opened the prize up to entries in every genre from poetry to short stories, from scripts to children's literature – rather than the usual one genre that changes every year – so we could support the widest range of creativity in such difficult conditions.

So in keeping, we've decided to offer something in the way of a creative dialogue, affording ourselves a prosthetic social opportunity at a time when social interaction has dramatically changed.

SP: Will, have you noticed any changes in your own work during lockdown?
Yes, certainly. Particularly when I think of how technology now shapes human conversation and human labour in novel ways, so that less time is wasted in commuting but more is spent fiddling with volume sliders and toggle settings, adjusting cameras and microphones and all the petty details forced upon us by Teams and Zoom. This is almost the world prophesied by E. M. Forster in "The Machine Stops", a short story from 1909. In Forster's world, all communication is remote. We're not yet in the dystopian underground bunkers of "The Machine Stops", thank goodness, but the switch to mass online communication has created subtle consequences that will ramify slowly and will take years or even decades to process. In my own field, universities are already working through the future implications of the enforced transition to online teaching. A permanent change to some form of remote learning, at least as an option, is probably inevitable, though seminars by Teams are arguably of less benefit to staff and students than face-to-face debate.

Foreword

WS: Si, how has your own writing gone in this strange time?
I know in terms of my own practice as a creative writer that everything has changed. Processes have been agitated, and outcomes. What has come out has correspondingly had a very different aesthetic. I'm in a band called The Loose Kites and instead of writing typically formatted song lyrics, a great deal of what I've been putting down – now normally on my phone instead of paper – has been poetic one-liners.

This has largely come about due to the wanders I try to take at the end of each day when I ruminate on what I see and think as I plod up the sandstone hills near where I live. The ups and downs of Cheshire's sedimentary backbone don't take kindly to nestling into an A4 paper and pencil, and besides I haven't wanted to stop my pathering. I'm not for one minute claiming to be a ridge-dwelling equivalent of Bashō, but this period of forced change has certainly benefitted my writing. You might say that the hills mirror the vicissitudes of recent experience. While it's been a period of suffering, I've come still closer to my home. I've let the landscape hold me. And I've tried to encapsulate that in ways I haven't tried before. I've certainly written more this year, and it seems the whole county has! We had a record number of submissions.

SP: Was this or anything else a surprise to you in the submissions?
The sheer number was not only a welcome surprise but also a healthy affirmation of the value of creative writing in such a time. I was impressed by how many submissions managed to find unusual angles from which to interpret lockdown. We had stories, poems and scripts set in science fictional contexts, in worlds of legend, and in dreams; and yet we also received many brutally real, contemporary visions of the pandemic, whose defamiliarising details and raw intensity carried the power to shock, despite the dull, repetitive banality of much of socially distanced, masked-up daily life.

It's also wonderful that the University of Chester is supporting such an important artistic venture at a time when urban myths are disseminated, in academia as well as in the press, of the limited value of the humanities to industry. These myths are not true, of course, as the best, most forward-thinking businesses will always particularly value staff who can write fluently, read critically and think independently. Thanks to the support of the University for the Prize, people can see for themselves what a strong role an outward-looking, socially engaged English Department can play for the local community and the national body of readers.

WS: What stood out for you about the submissions this year?
One other thing I'm certain of, is that the writing (and the walking) have been tremendous aids in looking after myself during this unsettling and difficult time. Writing has really helped me make sense of things. In recent years, I have felt privileged to work with Lapidus International, the organisation for writing for wellbeing. I can safely say that never before has their work seemed so personally poignant to me, and I think it would be fair to say that a clear strength of this year's submissions was the authenticity of the diverse voices coming through so much of the work, often wrangling with uncomfortable ideas, or disentangling unwanted feelings. Even if a piece seemed perhaps not so deftly crafted as one of its peers, very often the sheer genuineness of its tone would move me. For this reason alone, many of the submissions warranted careful consideration.

SP: Did you notice anything significant in this year's submissions, Will?
It was great to see people's creativity blossoming under this year's relentless pressure. Some of the submissions looked like the work of very experienced writers who were nevertheless finding new resources with which to comment on the terrible world around them. Other entries read like the work of people moved to pick up the pen for the first time but who were able, despite – or perhaps because of – these distressing and almost unprecedented circumstances, to give voice to profound emotions in poignant and memorable ways.

Foreword

Having read such a huge number of enjoyable, moving and uplifting entries, it was very difficult to pick winners. After much discussion, we and our fellow judges Linda Tyson and Alex Clifton – to whom huge thanks is due – eventually chose in each category the following to share the Cheshire Prize for Literature 2020: "A Rock Called Pluto" by Leon Coleman (short stories); "New Backgrounds" by Chris Nelson (children's literature); "Residue" by Paul Howarth (poetry); and "Home Sweet Home" by Caitlin Norbury (scriptwriting). We also chose one runner-up in each category: "Relative Humidity" by Esther Amis-Hughes (short stories); "Lockdown 2041" by Janys Chambers (children's literature); "Equinox 2020" by Maria Isakova-Bennett (poetry; not featured in this anthology by request of the poet); and "I Am Stars" by Julie McKiernan (scriptwriting). The anthology is arranged by genre, and the winners and runners-up appear at the beginning of each section.

So, on a final note, we would simply add a thank you, for all the hard work that our co-judges put in, given the sheer volume of the submissions, and for the unequivocal compassion of the work of all the entrants. Thanks also, to Storyhouse, and other colleagues for supporting the Cheshire Prize for Literature's continued development and the importance given to our shared cultural growth.

Si Poole, Storyhouse
William Stephenson, University of Chester

A ROCK CALLED PLUTO

Leon Coleman

Dad said I should leave you a voice memo. But I'm not sure what to say. It was sunny today and I had fish fingers. I know I always used to say that I can't wait till I move out. So, I could live on my own and not have to share with you. Cos you keep wearing my socks and undies. Which wouldn't be too bad cos they get washed, but you're older and a lot bigger than me, and … well, Mum says you're big boned, so they're all baggy when I get them back. And you keep farting, especially at night, and I'm on the top bunk, and fart air rises, so I get to whiff all your farts, but you don't get to whiff any of my mine. And that's not fair. And when I want to play *Minecraft*, but can't cos you're there, on the computer playing *Call of Duty* with people all over the world. And I can't even use the tablet cos you're taking all the internet and you're shouting stuff all over the world and they're giving it back. And I can't even listen to my music cos you're playing your music so loud it doesn't even sound like music, just some guy screaming like he's banged his toe or something. And I know you smoke, even though I've never seen you do it, but I can smell it on you, even though you try and cover it with Dad's aftershave, but I haven't told Mum, even though I could have, loads of times. And I think you smoke other stuff too, cos I've seen it in your shoe, a little plastic bag with stuff that looks like dry herbs. And you're always saying I'm wrong when I say stuff. Like that time Dad was taking us to Grandma's and Dad asked me how many planets there were, and I said there were nine, and then you said I was wrong, that they'd found out that Pluto wasn't a real planet, just a stupid rock you said. Which seems weird to me. That Pluto's gone from being a planet and now is just a rock. It hasn't changed, but the way we think about it has. And the times you said you wish I was never born. That you never wanted a little brother. You said that loads of times. And when you were saying it I was thinking, well you're not so great to live with either. And you kept saying I was too little to

Unlocked

understand stuff, even though I understand loads of stuff. And I said I wish you would move out, and you said one day you would.

And then everything started to change. It was on the news, the Prime Minister with the weird hair was talking. And Mum and Dad looked worried. Mum was asking him about it and he kept saying how the hell would he know and why wouldn't she just let him listen. I hate this stupid Covid or Corona or whatever it's called. Mum and Dad said you weren't allowed out to meet your friends anymore and said we had to stay inside all the time. That we could only go out with them. You said you'd rather stay inside then. But then after bedtime you got up, you told me your girlfriend was upset and that you had to see her to make sure she was all right. So, you sneaked out and you made me promise not to say anything and I promised I wouldn't. But then you went out every other night as well. Even though Dad told us we couldn't go out, no matter what, especially you because of your diabetes. But you're not that diabetic. You eat crisps and Haribo every day. I said it was dangerous to go out, but you said it was okay. You said young people don't get Covid or Corona or whatever it's called. You said that it's only old people that get sick. But that's not true. And I didn't say anything, to Mum or Dad about you going out, but now I wish I did.

And now you're not here, and to be honest it's weird getting used to the room being so quiet. Being so tidy. I can hear Mum in the bedroom crying. Dad's cleared out the loft and fixed everything in the house. Now he's always in the garage. He keeps taking the bikes apart and putting them together again. He says he's fixed the gear problem you had. Said it was the ray lor or something. He said it will ride like a new bike for when you come back. I pretend I don't know what's going on. But I do. I go on the internet and talk with friends, on FaceTime and Skype and Zoom. Rex is missing you lots too. When Dad grabs the lead, Rex runs to our bedroom. I'm sure he's looking for you cos he runs there even when I'm at the front door with my coat on waiting. I know you didn't like taking him on walks, but I think he liked you taking him. And I liked coming along with you both. My

A Rock Called Pluto

favourite bit was when you'd find a stick and hold it high then swing it over your head, like you were throwing it really far. Rex would go shooting off and then stop, confused, wondering where the stick had gone, but you'd hidden the stick behind your back. I tried to do it too but never fooled Rex like you did.

It was my birthday yesterday, I'm eight now, so I'm only seven behind you. Mum made a chocolate cake, my favourite. I would bring you some, but you're not allowed visitors, and anyway, you're diabetic. It's weird to imagine you there, in a hospital, lying down, far away, with other patients around you, with machines helping them breathe, the same machines that are helping you breathe. Mum says that they put you to sleep, so you don't know what's happening, that you're probably having good dreams and that you'll probably be home soon. Dad says we just have to wait. So, every day we hope we get some good news. Dad says no news is good news.

Anyway, it's time to sleep now. I hope you get better and come home soon. If you come back, I promise I won't moan about your farts, or you wearing my undies and socks. And I won't moan about you playing *Call of Duty*, even with all those weird American guys swearing all the time. But the music, well, okay, you can play the music, even though it is horrible.

I was reading today about Pluto and what the scientists thought about it all. They said Pluto was different because it was really far away and on its side. They also said it wasn't a real planet because it couldn't get away from the other smaller rocks following it around in space. But maybe it doesn't want to get away from those smaller rocks. Maybe for those smaller rocks, Pluto is a planet, and not just another rock. But a rock called Pluto.

RELATIVE HUMIDITY

Esther Amis-Hughes

Graeme was telling me (again) about his divorce when I noticed the leopard's ear. He realised that I'd stopped pretending to listen and followed my gaze.

"That ear. It was attached before, wasn't it?" You start to imagine things when you check an empty building this often. Graeme leant closer to the glass case. He tilted his head to one side and made a sort of guttural sound. Graeme's noises were the only live human sounds I'd heard for three months.

"I think I'd remember if it only had one ear. We'll email the curators."

We finished our check of the gallery – the other animals seemed to have all their bits in the right places – and headed up to the security office to log our report.

This was the longest the museum had been closed in its 149-year history. The head curator loved to tell us that it even stayed open during the War. The pandemic seemed to be defeating many things the War couldn't. Still, sitting on our arses watching Netflix was hardly a hardship, as Graeme liked to say. He was a military history fanatic (of course he was) and had waited his whole life for a global emergency. The fact that one had occurred which didn't require an instant armed response was a source of bitterness to him.

We had a reply from the curator the next night. He had forwarded our email to one of the conservators who had requested all the humidity readings.

"I mean a divorce in lockdown? Who even does that?" Graeme had an extraordinary knack of starting every conversation in the middle. I suspected it was because he didn't need an audience and spoke even when I wasn't there.

Relative Humidity

I logged onto the environmental system and checked the Relative Humidity tab. A graph opened up and Graeme leaned over my shoulder to look. He smelt of fried food and Lynx. I moved to the side.

"Two metres, Graeme."

The graph showed the relative humidity over the last six months. January, February and March were pretty stable at around 48%; but suddenly in April it dropped and kept dropping. Since the lockdown, graphs documented our entire lives. Deaths, infection, recession. They'd taken on a sinister new narrative meaning. This graph was no different. The slow plummet in April continued into May and June, where it was now at 28% and still dropping.

I clicked the forward command and sent the chart to the conservator. It unsettled me. I felt like a custodian of this stuff. Not a key worker exactly, but I was proud that I was still allowed into the building when even the curators, those lofty academics who had their names on books, weren't. When all this madness was over, people would want to return to the things they used to enjoy. We had to keep everything safe until then.

I realised Graeme had briefly left the topic of his ex as we started that night's checks.

"Closed. Can you believe it? Cinemas? I tell you, we'll be next. We aren't essential."

"I dunno. People need history. And knowledge."

"No way. I'm telling you, it's over for this place. This crap just isn't relevant."

"Does it need to be relevant, though? Isn't being interesting or beautiful enough? Or being a window into the past? Think of the school kids that used to visit before all this."

"Schools? They won't be coming on trips! Imagine the risk assessments. Or the catching up they'll be doing for 'real' subjects. You're talking about the past. This the future. Pandemics. Global warming. Terrorism."

Unlocked

We logged the further damage to the leopard, whose other ear had cracked, and submitted our reports. As Graeme set the alarms on the top floor, I did a quick internet search on relative humidity:

Organic collections (such as wood, paper, fur, feathers, bones) need an environment with stable relative humidity, ideally between 40% and 70%. Should the relative humidity rise above 70%, there is a risk collections will grow mould. Should it fall below 40%, organic artefacts will release some of their own moistures into the air. Over a long period of time this could result in objects becoming dry and even cracking.

The conservator replied the next day. The email had a little red exclamation mark by it, indicating its urgency. The conservator was very worried about the data. The collections were at risk, relative humidity had never dropped this low. If the cause wasn't immediately identified and slowly rectified (no sudden changes please!), the whole gallery, indeed the whole museum would be at risk. I scanned through the email, impatient to find the solution. He signed off with an apology that he couldn't come in himself. The Trust was crippled by debt after being closed for so long, and it had decided to immediately furlough all non-essential staff. Neither conservator nor curator would be available until further notice.

I shut down the email.

"Graeme!" Where was he now? "All the other staff have been furloughed." That made him reappear.

"Off work with pay? Bloody hell. It's so unfair." He stropped around getting the keys ready for our check.

"Conservator reckons something has changed the relative humidity. That's why the animals have started breaking. We need to figure out what's changed. Will you go look at the heating plant room and check the system is on the same configuration? It might have needed an update or something."

Relative Humidity

Graeme stomped out, still muttering. I got out the logbooks to check if any maintenance should have been done, but it all looked fine. I pulled up the air unit report on the system, the temperature graphs were more or less stable. So what had changed since March?

Graeme announced his return, kicking the office door open.

"Plant room fine, no changes there. Come on, let's do our checks. If everyone else is on holiday, I don't see why we should stick around here."

We walked round the gallery, Graeme mumbling about how he'd spend furlough if he had it. As far as I could tell it involved a chat room and some fan fiction.

We walked past the huge elephant skull which gazed at the museum entrance all day, welcoming visitors with a faraway look. Or it used to. More sad news in the gallery itself. The swooping macaws were visibly wilting and three of the chimp's ribs were cracked on the left side, where its heart would have been.

We photographed the new damage, but there was no one to send it to now all the staff were furloughed.

That night I returned to the internet, searching for other museums with the same problem. I found a collections care chat room.

latercurator: anyone having issues with relative humidity and collections?
ilovedinos: yup, bones cracking here in mid-west US
DublinLocalHist: some of our paper and wood items are drying out
Artlover: our picture frames have started to warp, some of them are cracking
latercurator: anyone know what's going on. All our temp data is ok.
FriendofGreta: GLOBAL WARMING isn't anyone listening?
DublinLocalHist: get away with you FriendofGreta. This is a sudden change, something since lockdown.
Artlover: same here, this only started when all the galleries were shut. WHY?

latercurator: not sure it matters anyway. We just got word, they're looking at closing the museum.
DublinLocalHist: Same here. Curators all redundant as of last week.
Artlover: I can't believe this. All this stuff. All this knowledge. It's short sighted.
latercurator: :(

I flicked through the rest of the chat. There was no answer. But all these other places were having the same problem. All their objects were showing damage too. Why?

The Middlewich Metro
15 September 2020
The doors of Middlewich Natural History Museum closed for the final time today. Middlewich Heritage Trust, which runs the museum and other local sites of interest, entered administration last Friday, stating that without considerable financial assistance it could no longer afford to pay its staff when the furlough scheme ends. The collections are likely to be auctioned to private collectors but like many museums, the Natural History Museum has reported damage to several objects as a result of a dramatic fall in relative humidity. Last week, after extensive damage was discovered in two galleries at the British Museum, a report from Imperial College London found that extreme environmental change in the country's galleries was due to the lack of visitors. A spokesman said "chattering people literally breathe life into our galleries. The droplets of water they expel when they breathe and talk provide the vital conditions for our heritage to survive. Without people, our history and culture is dying." The final post on the Museum's Instagram account is of "Nelly", the elephant skull who famously greeted all visitors for 149 years. Our last view of Nelly shows a huge crack running from the inside corner of her left eye, all the way down to her mouth.

ONE FOSSIL TO ANOTHER

Sheila Tyrer Hughes

August 2020. So far, a year to remember – and not for the best of reasons. But, amid the hardship, sadness and discontent, business for Herbert Stapleton had been good. So good in fact that in sympathy for the bereaved he had cut his prices drastically. Normally professional and detached – *now* he was tired and depressed. Now, he decided, was the time to give in to the twinges in his back, to change hats and plan for the future, in the hope that one day soon, before age defeated him, a new future would emerge – and he would realise his wildest, craziest dream.

He picked up his Bible and opened it to a well-thumbed page.

Numbers 23, verse 22: "He hath as it were the strength of a unicorn."

Herbert Stapleton belonged to another age entirely. He'd always appeared old to those of nodding acquaintance – ever since he was twenty-five and had become the sole proprietor of Stapleton, Boggis and Stapleton, funeral directors. That was in 1975. Now, aged seventy and a half, after four of the busiest months he had ever known, he had given mortality a serious thought and sold the business to the first takers, a couple of young upstarts in their forties who, he suspected, would never give the job quite the respect and attention to detail that it deserved.

For several weeks he had been training them and in fairness they seemed keen to do well, but he hadn't failed to notice the raised eyebrows, the shared ironic look, the coughs, and twitches as they attempted to hide smiles. He knew what they thought of him. A dry old stick. Out of date, out of time. They were polite and agreeable enough, but he knew they would change things, update his methods, modernise his techniques. How can you modernise a funeral and maintain that degree of gravitas and sincerity necessary for a dignified service? Death is death, after all. Nothing modern about that. It's a serious business. Black is the order of the day. He couldn't do with all that frivolity. Pop tunes playing in the crematorium. Women in jeans or jogging bottoms, men without ties.

He showed them the black beribboned top-hats and the tailcoat his father wore until his death as he walked the last 200 yards of the coffin's journey in front of the hearse. He showed them his own suits, the pride of his wardrobe, made to measure in Carnaby Street: his shirts with their starched removable collars – and his shoes, polished to such a finish you could practically see your reflection in the leather. He showed them the sponges and the chamois leathers he used to clean the cars. He interviewed them as if they were the bereaved, using his gentle, reassuring tones, without condescension or insincerity. A bereaved family had to know that he would take care of everything.

And he had. Always. Just as his father had. In over seventy years they had never had a single complaint.

They thought he was hard of hearing. They thought ... Hm! He wasn't at all hard of hearing. He wasn't any of the things they thought he was. He was just preoccupied sometimes, lost in his own thoughts. It amused him to listen to their whispered undertones as they prepared a client for his last journey and *he* was busy with the books. They giggled about Dickens a lot. Uriah Heep, Ebenezer Scrooge and Tite Barnacle were names he regularly heard. He let them prattle on and smiled inwardly. At least it meant they were literate – and he understood the initial need for diversion when preparing a client for burial. Still, he did have to look up Tite Barnacle. Turns out he and other members of the Barnacle family controlled the Circumlocution Office in Dickens's *Little Dorrit*, the purpose of which was to prevent things being done and to demonstrate "how *not* to do it".

Well, he had shown them how it *should* be done. He could do no more. His duty to his father and grandfather was at an end.

"Now," he told them on his last day, "like Mrs Barkis, I am 'going out with the tide'." And out he went.

One Fossil to Another

He knew they would be wondering what he would do with his life. He had lived for death. Now perhaps, death would be his only option. There was no Mrs Stapleton, no little Stapletons. His home was a bungalow, neat and symmetrical, the garden small: manicured lawn edged with heathers. They would imagine him alone, drinking Ovaltine watching daytime television, sinking slowly into a slough of despond. They would imagine the completion of the desiccation process until all that was left of Herbert was dust. They couldn't be more wrong.

Herbert Stapleton was on a mission.

On account of a grateful customer, he had a mystery to solve. The funeral business had been a demanding one. It had left no time for holidays even, let alone the pursuit of mysteries and adventures. That final day at the funeral parlour ended with Herbert Stapleton at home alone packing away everything that belonged to his past life. Each item and article of clothing was meticulously folded, wrapped in tissue paper, boxed and carried into the roof space of the bungalow. As he hauled up the last of the boxes he remembered a day in the fifties when, though very young, he had watched a programme called *Buried Treasure* on their new television. It was about stones. Not tomb stones. Much, much bigger: stones that were transported 160 miles from the Preseli hills to the Salisbury Plain. And it was about people solving mysteries, searching for clues, delving into the past.

When he was fourteen, Herbert Stapleton had wanted to be an archaeologist.

His hero was Sir Mortimer Wheeler, 1954's TV celebrity of the year and one of the stars of *Buried Treasure*. But in 1964 you didn't always get what you wanted. Henry Stapleton was determined his son would follow him into the business, just as he had followed his own father, another Herbert. It was secure, reliable, a good living. There would always be a demand. And Herbert couldn't argue with that.

Still, he had kept his interest in stones and bones, in history and the mysteries that still survived. His home was a shrine to his obsession. He had read and researched for years, wondering how he would spend his considerable wealth. Which teasing trail would he pursue? Now he had the answer in the palm of his hand.

The grateful customer in the 1990s had been a man of independent means. After a Cambridge education he had spent thirty years exploring the lesser known nooks and crannies of the world. He had come home to roost in his mid-fifties and had been married for a mere seven years when he and Herbert met over the business of his wife's funeral. Thereafter, they had become friends of sorts and Finn McClure, an adventurer's name if ever there was one, regaled him with accounts of his many and varied exploits. To cut short what became a long and sometimes tedious part of Herbert's story, on McClure's death five years ago he left Herbert a collection of photographs and a stone.

It was that same stone that Herbert now held in his hand. He had shown it to no one. They would only laugh, consider him eccentric, crazy even.

The photograph that lay before him was of a man who was himself holding up a photograph. On close examination, the photograph appeared to be of a cave painting, a strange animal, a hybrid of deer and horse. From its forehead sprouted a single tapering horn. On the back of the photograph were the words Lago Posadas, Patagonia.

That's where he would begin.

And the stone. Well, not just a stone. Within it, a strange fragment, a fine conical shape two centimetres in diameter at one end tapering to a fine point with faint, spiral indentations.

Herbert smiled as he stroked it with his thumb.

"Just think of it, Stapleton," McClure had said. "Finding proof that the unicorn is more than just a myth."

Whispering "He hath as it were the strength of a unicorn" over and over, he unwrapped his new rucksack and began to pack.

When this crazy world finally got back to normal Herbert Stapleton, retired funeral director, dry old stick, and believer in unicorns, would be ready.

THE CRAFT

Jennifer Gray

There's a rowan at the bottom of the garden. I can see it from the kitchen sink or when I look down from our bedroom window. The way it bends in the breeze, the ballast of berries bright in the autumn air.

I grew up in this house, long before the virus. Long before any of this. I always loved the garden, the largest one on the estate, running downhill to the stream. If you squint from here you can see into the dark of the coppice beyond. From my seat at the table, I watch the shadows shift. There is something hiding in the woods.

Then the front door clicks, and I know he's home.

I stay in mostly, we all have to now. I've been making Christmas cards, using dress-making scissors to cut out jolly robins. Their red breasts are bright, the hue of rowan berries. Those trees, they say they keep the witches away. And is it vampires who can't cross running water?

He washes his hands in the sink when he comes back from the shops, he sings "Happy Birthday" out loud, or recites "The Owl and Pussycat" as water thunders out of the tap. He says he does it to protect me. I sit at the table and wonder if he will one day drop the act and count to thirty in his head like the rest of us.

I didn't marry an ordinary man, though. I married Joel. He's never done anything by halves. Ask him to buy Marmite and he comes back from Tesco with three jars. *It will take a year to eat all those.* I've given up saying it. And when we first met he dressed all in black like a highwayman. *I can change his wardrobe.* I thought to myself. *He's a good man. He's a kind man.* But it turns out you never know people, not really.

I bought you some more cardboard for your arty-farty crafts. Joel lays a coloured packet on the kitchen top and leans to kiss the top of my head. I don't know if he senses the shiver, but he stiffens and pulls away. He goes into the other room, opens a beer. I hear the clink of the bottle cap as it hits the wooden floor and skids under the couch.

Outside night is falling fast, the momentum of the year is pulling down the daylight, eventually even the leaves will turn black. My eye is caught again by the rowan, and I'm drawn to the window. Looking out at the brightness of those berries, startling in the last of the light, and then, prickling with the hot animal instinct of dread, the hairs on my arms stand on end.

There's a figure standing just below the tree, she's clothed in black, long hair whipped back by the wind. Compelled, I move towards the glass, my nose so close to the cold pane that I see it fog with my quickened breath. When I wipe the glass with my sleeve, she is gone.

It's later, Joel is in the kitchen, starting on dinner. When he first moved in, he never cooked. He wanted me to play housewife. Now I don't get near the recipe books, let alone the chopping board. He has taken all control: what he buys with his money, what we watch on TV. I can hear his voice. *You look tired tonight, lay your head here, I'm going to pick us out something.* And he strokes my hair as I lay in his lap, teeth gritted, waiting, clock watching like I did in school. Except now there's no breaktime, and the day doesn't end, it simply blurs unfolding into another version of the same dreaded day.

He took the lock off the bathroom door when he moved in. *No secrets here, Janine. What's mine is yours.* A wink. What a stroke of good luck for him when the government put us into lockdown. *Stay home, save lives.* The panic tightened in my chest like a snare. The other night I put a chair under the door handle in the bedroom to see if it would keep him away. The next day he broke it up and burned it for firewood. Now I leave my clothes in a heap on the floor.

He hums as we eat, tapping his foot to Johnny Cash. *Love is a burning thing.* We played this song at our wedding. Joel puts his fork down and smiles at me. *You're truly beautiful Janine. Perfection. I can't wait to show you off to the world again.* I know this sinking feeling well. *Down, down, down ...*

The Craft

I take our plates, scrub them in the sink, all the while keeping one eye on the garden. It's too dark now, I can't see the stream or the woods beyond, the rowan is just a whip of black. The moon is hiding behind charcoal clouds, but I know it's there. Just like I know she's there.

He is spooned around me on the couch as we watch *Top Gun*. Joel lives for the vicarious adrenaline rush. Back when there were aeroplanes in the sky, that could have been him. I know the storyline well, but tonight it feels different, loaded somehow. I mouth the famous lines. *That's right, Iceman. I am dangerous.* I can feel him harden against me, the patriotic pull and thrust of skin on steel is all too much.

In the bathroom, I brush my teeth so hard my gums bleed. I watch the blood loop round the porcelain. I imagine there is more of it. I Imagine I could turn the taps and run a sinkful. He's still downstairs, but he'll be up soon, it's nearly midnight.

I tread downstairs quietly. In the living room he coughs, but the wind is up and the house is old, I flow through it like cool air. He invaded my home ground, and knowing the territory is the only upper hand I have now. Not a soul knows the tread of these floorboards better … the howl of the chimney covers for me like a friend.

I take the crafting card from the tabletop, tuck it under my arm. Then my hand goes back to the surface and runs over the scissors, the spooled handles and perfect end. The point of it all.

Tonight then, I'll let her in.

When I go upstairs again, I draw back the curtains, sit on the cool windowsill. Outside the trees in the coppice bend with the will of the wind, the garden is shifting under the light of a swollen moon. Somewhere out there a fox whoops and cackles, an owl hoots, there are players waiting in the wings.

The first raindrops hit the window as he treads the stairs. *I'm coming up darling, ready or not.* He laughs at his own wonderful wit, but the boards creak their objection beneath his heavy step. I feel cold steel in the sleeve of my dressing gown. *Oh, I'm ready, baby.*

At the bedroom door he pauses. *Knock. Knock.* One last absurdity. The handle turns, he doesn't wait for me to invite him in. Only the

Unlocked

undead have those kinds of manners. Joel steps into the bedroom, he's already begun unbuttoning his shirt, but his fingers falter.

What are you doing out of bed? Come on, it's freezing in here. He sits on the edge of the mattress and pats the duvet cover, patiently at first. I don't move, arms neatly folded, sitting in the window. Joel's face drops, disappointment. He slaps the bed and rises to his feet.

What the fuck are you looking at Janine? It's pitch black out there.

I've turned back towards the glass. Below, in the garden, there is movement. The clouds drift and suddenly, a burst of moonlight ignites the lawn. At last, she emerges from the trees like a spectre. Her bare arms and legs are streaked with soil, her wet, black hair is a twist of rope down her back.

My hand is on the latch.

Don't even think about it. He crosses the room in three quick strides.

Below the woman bends her arm skyward to catch the rain, the mud runs from her skin. Before Joel can stop me, I throw the window wide. He's shouting above the wind, his hand on my neck, fingernails in my scalp, and then the full weight of him is on me. For one sharp second, I feel fear.

And then the heat of his blood.

I hold his head up so he can see through the glass, though his eyes grow duller by the second. My lap is slippery with his blood, and I think that these stains won't come out. Joel sighs, as if impatient, and then he leaves me, his neck wound gaping, his eyes wide.

The window bangs shut. Once again, the garden is empty.

THE REALLY GOOD BOOK CLUB PAPERS

Rebecca Kershaw

Being a record of the meetings of the Really Good Book Club kept by myself, Secretary of the Club.

February 2020
***Don't Know What You've Got Till it's Gone* by Gemma Crisp.**
Score – 7/10
Present – Rachel, Magda, Andrea, Christophe, myself. Apologies, Rose. After a slightly lacklustre debate around the book, reflected in that deadliest of scores, seven, Rachel produced her strawberry layer cake. Then we got down to the real discussions – books we're reading which aren't for book club, TV recommendations and holiday plans. As usual Magda has lots arranged. We are in awe of her ability to track down a bargain. Slovenia and Venice are on her schedule so far. Rachel has tickets to *Coriolanus* and there was much discussion about the best place to eat and whether that should be pre or post show. Andrea asked what we thought of the chatter about this new virus. As you might expect Christophe had never heard of it, whereas Magda seemed to have been tracking its progress in minute detail. Rachel wished everyone would stop using the word "lockdown". "It's so American. We don't do lockdowns in Britain." Agreed to meet at Christophe's next month on the understanding he'll make chilli chocolate brownies and doesn't have to finish the book.

March
***This is Going to Hurt* by Adam Kay.**
8/10
Group meeting temporarily by email. Chilli chocolate brownies on hold. The last four days have been spent exchanging messages as to whether the meeting should go ahead. Much use of words like "contagion", "risk" and Rachel's beloved "lockdown". Group split between Rachel, Christophe and me, who wanted to meet, Rose who was "easy either

way" and Magda and Andrea who said better not. Decided to leave it this month and have a get together online. Not very successful to be honest. No one wanted to discuss the book. Christophe concerned he has thirty-eight chilli chocolate brownies which he and Leon will now need to eat. I asked why thirty-eight but he didn't seem to know.

April
***Lockdown* by Peter May**
9/10
Meeting online. All present though it's fair to say some more present than others. Rose, that's you I'm talking about. Although it does feel as though we've been in a perpetual meeting since the 23 March. So many emails! So many WhatsApp groups and funny (?) videos! I feel I need to bury my phone to stop those flipping notification pings. Anyway, we're online until this lockdown (even Rachel has accepted that's what it is) is lifted. Christophe says he's not making any more brownies. It apparently took him and Leon two weeks to eat them all and they've each put on a stone in weight. Can't just be down to the brownies, surely?

May
***Zoom* by Istvan Banyai**
We've abandoned scoring for the duration. Attempting the book is now considered sufficient.

So, a Zoom meeting. It was by no means a unanimous decision to go "on camera" and I don't believe there'll be the appetite for it again. To be honest I get quite enough playing *Celebrity Squares* with work meetings and by the time everyone had finished shouting "can you hear me" and trying to explain how to unmute and turn the camera on there wasn't a lot of energy left for discussing the book. Which, as it was a picture book, didn't matter too much. See how our standards have fallen. Can't even manage words.

June
In Praise of Walking by Shane O'Mara
Back to an email group and a giant sigh of relief from most members. I have a sneaking suspicion Rose and Magda did their own little Zoom meeting without the rest of us but as long as I don't have to watch myself watching everyone else that's fine by me. It seems that the entire neighbourhood is out walking. Certainly, everyone in the group pulls on the hiking boots and marches forth at least once a day. Andrea and Rose have started meeting up for walks which is nice. Things are looking brighter all round, tentative talk of days out. Rachel has ventured to some newly opened gardens and Andrea is planning on a trip to the coast. Such excitement at the thought of a glimpse of the sea and the taste of Mr Whippy ice cream. Christophe says he will make an ice cream cake for next month but as none of us will be eating it he didn't receive the praise he was clearly expecting.

July
Bubble by Stewart Foster
Tonight, we started compiling a lockdown lexicon. Who would have thought "bubble" would ever need a new definition? In other news Rachel has been to a restaurant! Where once we would have asked about the extent of the menu and the quality of the food tonight the questions were "how safe did it feel? Did the staff have masks or visors?" But the fact remains that Rachel has been OUT FOR A MEAL SHE DIDN'T COOK HERSELF. Christophe's photos of the promised ice cream cake were quite overshadowed.

August
The Restaurant: A History of Eating Out by William Sitwell
And now we're all at it! Eating Out to Help Out is an actual thing where you get to eat at lots of lovely restaurants for half price and while you are savouring your asparagus risotto you can feel worthy because you are officially HELPING OUT. So, tonight's group was all about where we'd been and what we'd eaten and where we'd recommend next. It's like we've all returned to the real world. Or the world has returned to

us, I'm not sure which. There's even talk of GOING ON HOLIDAY. In other news Christophe has stopped baking because he says it's cheaper to eat someone else's cakes.

September
***Quarantine* by Jim Crace**
Andrea is self-isolating. Her app pinged and now she has to stay at home for fourteen days or ten days or eleven depending who you ask. It certainly put an end to our discussions about whether we should meet in person this month. Rachel had offered her barn and there was lots of agreement about not sharing cars and bringing our own flasks and cakes and measuring tapes and is it two metres or one metre plus or something else. Anyway, then Andrea's app pinged. So here we are online. Christophe sent photos of Leon's Cherry Bakewell. I think it was supposed to cheer us up but instead it made my Mr Kipling's Battenburg look quite inadequate.

October
***One Hundred Years of Solitude* by Gabriel Garcia Marquez**
Tiers or Tears? A very subdued group tonight. Everyone had read the book but maybe it would have been better if we hadn't. The sunny days of Eating Out and Helping Out seem a long time ago. Walking isn't as much fun in the rain. The WhatsApp groups are quiet. Christophe made gingerbread men but even they have glum faces.

November
***Forever and a Day* by Anthony Horowitz**
Lockdown 2.0. Even James Bond would have struggled with it this time. Will we ever meet again in person? Will we ever visit another book shop? Would I remember what to do if I did? Christophe and Leon are fasting. Just when I could do with a picture of one of their ridiculous confections. At least the twinkling lights of Christmas are ahead of us.

December
***Christmas is Cancelled* by Aurelia B. Rowl**
Maybe the twinkling lights are dimmed BUT Christophe baked his special boozy mince pies and DELIVERED THEM TO US AT HOME, along with one of those little bottles of wine each and a Christmas napkin with a cheerful plum pudding on it. We all raised a glass to the end of 2020 and the hope of meetings to come. We decided we will only read happy books next year.

January 2021
***A Journal of the Plague Year* by Daniel Defoe**
Okay, so last year's resolution to read only happy books has already fallen by the wayside. But is it any wonder? Nonetheless a certain stoicism has entered us this year. Everyone had read the book, everyone contributed to the discussion, everyone was upbeat and determined to keep on keeping on. It was Christophe's birthday last week and Leon had baked him a three-tier cake – very appropriate we thought. Sadly, the restrictions meant he couldn't bring us each a slice round but we sang "happy birthday" and talked about vaccines. All in all, a satisfactory start to the year.

February
***Ordinary People in Extraordinary Times* by Nancy Bermeo**
The anniversary of our last "real" meeting. We have given up planning our reunion and are just enjoying each meeting as it comes. Christophe baked chilli chocolate brownies in honour of the occasion and posted them to us. Rather surprisingly they all arrived in time, some slightly squashed but the thought, and the flavour, was there. We agreed a list of books for the next twelve months so no matter what happens we'll keep on reading. Cheers.

LEAVING ROOM FOR GOD'S WRATH

Nicola Russell Johnson

Being a social worker sort of happens when you're not looking. It creeps up on you. Like eczema. In my case, it's because my mother spent my entire life telling me I was too stupid to achieve anything, so I went off and did a degree, pretty much to spite her. We didn't have the best of relationships. You know, when you're an only child and still not the favourite, it can leave a mark. Still, with me out the house she had more room for gin, so I suppose we both got what we wanted. There I was, twenty-one, fresh out of uni and the only jobs going were at the local supermarket or with the council. BAM, suddenly I'm a social worker.

I've spent the last twenty years in work thinking, why didn't I pick the supermarket?

A nice clean supermarket, with nice clean people.

You'd be horrified at what I've seen.

Shit.

Actual shit. On people's carpets. I mean they actually just let their dogs shit on the floor and don't clean it up. Then they proudly tell you how much better they've been doing and how they've done all the stuff you asked and the whole time there's just a massive turd on the floor.

One house, the toilet blocked up, and instead of plunging it or calling a plumber, they just started crapping into sandwich bags and tying them up. Then, because clearly, they wanted to make some small effort, they dumped the bags into the clogged toilet, until it became a small mountain of poo filled sandwich bags. And as I stood there in disbelief, they asked if I'd like a cup of tea. A cup of tea! I don't want a cup of tea, Beverly, there's a turd on the carpet.

I like to think I'm good with people though. And I've worked right through lockdown so far, so I'm doing my part. And you get to be a pretty good judge of character after a while. It'd take more than a fake plaster cast to get me stuffed into Ted Bundy's trunk.

I tell you what, I do a lot of work in old folks' homes, and I saw that doctor once. You know the one; he killed a bunch of old people and said it was heart attacks. I walked past him in the hallway and there was a cart full of minestrone in the way so he had to squeeze close and thinking back to it now, I got a really sinister vibe off him. You know, the way you feel when you watch old episodes of *Top of the Pops*.

That's where I'm heading today. I know, am I a hero or what? I'm going into an old folks' home during a pandemic. They'd better clap for me next Thursday because I'm widdling myself about it. I mean the Covid is why I'm going. And frankly if I had my way, I'd be in a full-on hazmat suit à la *ET* but instead all I've got is a disposable mask that's on its third wear and a bin bag with a head hole cut out.

To be fair, there aren't any confirmed cases in this home, but there was a nasty bout of impetigo and the lady who owns the home panicked and shut the place down. My job is to get the old dears shacked up with whatever family's nearest with a downstairs loo.

Mr Digby in room seventeen is my first go at it. We've contacted his son, an insurance advisor two towns over. Then I've got Mrs Jones and Mrs Dowding in rooms four and twenty-three. If all goes well, I'll get through about six of them by tomorrow. The rest should have family coming to get them. With any luck we'll have Dunkirked the entire place in about three days.

Mr Digby's son wasn't keen when I phoned him up yesterday, but he came round and he didn't sound like the sort who shits in a sandwich bag, so it should go well. I've just got to make a note of his medication as apparently there's a cyst in his arse-crack that's Mr Digby the younger's problem now.

When I show up to his room, he looks all right. Not exactly Sean Connery, but then neither's Sean Connery anymore, I suppose, so that's an unfair expectation. His clothes are bundled up in shopping bags. The staff help to stuff him into a wee stained wheelchair, and

Unlocked

I shout at him with as much cheeriness as I can: "THAT'S YOU ALL DONE, MR DIGBY!"

Mr Digby grunts at us. He's got snooker on the telly and he watches it the whole time I'm jamming his feet into slippers. His eyes are either a lovely pale blue colour or he's got cataracts. And he's still got lovely thick hair, albeit white ... and coming out of his ears.

Turns out though, he's a grumpy old git. I found that out while wheeling him over a cobblestone car park that made him rock like Hitler on meth. It takes two of us to get him into the car but soon enough I've got the windows down and Elaine Paige playing and we're going as fast as is possible without setting the speed cameras off. I read somewhere that lemon juice rubbed on your number plate means cameras can't see it. I wonder if it'd work with Piers Morgan's face.

When we get there, it's a nice, detached house in a cul-de-sac. It's the kind of place where you can get two bathrooms, a large garden, and a privet, all for a low price because next door has two rusting cars and a fridge-freezer on the drive.

Mr Digby's son answers the door in a mustard cardigan and behind him the house looks clean. He's wearing a mask too which I appreciate as his dad's hacked up onion smelling phlegm the entire car journey. My bin bag PPE has got to be covered in it. In fact, he coughs up a lung as we're bundling him into the house and setting him up in a chair by the telly. His son turns it on and one of those house-moving TV shows is on. You know the kind: Mr Jones is a door-to-door hamster salesman, Mrs Jones is a professional Princess Margaret impersonator, yet somehow, they've a budget of £450,000.

There's a small notebook on the table and Mr Digby's son goes over and pats it and then he says something lovely. He tells his dad that he's kept his secret diary from when he was nine and they're going to recreate it day by day. He says it'll be fun. He takes the forms I need signed, heads into the kitchen for a pen and I'm left watching the Joneses discuss the attraction of a converted gasworks in Crawley.

Leaving Room for God's Wrath

I peer over at the faded little notebook, and I don't know ... I get a weird feeling about it. It doesn't look like a diary or a cherished notebook. It looks like an old schoolbook that's been stolen and stuffed under floorboards. One of the stains doesn't sit right and I don't like the way Mr Digby's gone still.

I don't usually pry, but I pick it up and open it to a random page. It's written in pencil and a child's spidery hand.

6 July – Dad beat me with the extension lead and locked me in the cupboard. No food today but I'd hid a jar of water in there, so it wasn't so bad.

Mr Digby's son comes in as I'm reading, and he freezes. The signed papers are in his hands. I glance back at the old man, his gnarled fingers gripping the arms of his chair, and imagine how he must have looked forty years ago, bearing down on a small child with an electrical cord. I grab the forms off him, my heart pounding, and say "I'm sure everything's in order." Then I get the hell out. I climb into the car, tear off my mask and drive until I hit an empty pub car park. My hands are shaking, and I can't work out for the life of me what I'm actually feeling outside of panic.

That's when my manager rings. It's that call that we all dread. She tells me the cook from the old folks' home just tested positive. I'm to isolate for two weeks. My PPE is potentially saturated with the virus, as am I. She says I need to rush home, shower, and hole up and she offers to bring me some milk and a six-pack of baked beans.

And just like that I feel calm.

I know I should be worrying, but I do Zumba in my front room three times a week and I've got the lungs of a racehorse. In fact, what I'm suddenly thinking, is that I've got just enough petrol to stop off at my mother's house first ...

STILL LIFE

Matthew Rushton

Erin closed, making sure not to slam, the front door, and zipping up her black parka jacket walked down the road and away from the house. The night was cold and her breath hung in the air. Moonlight settled onto the tops and curved edges of cars parked outside the row of terrace houses. Moving through an alley she glimpsed momentarily the lives of others in well-lit kitchens, the backs of heads on colourful sofas, saw shadows play on lounge walls that changed blue, white, deep red and then black in television light.

She had no specific destination, just needed to *clear her head,* and *have some time by herself.* All he'd said in response was take your phone.

Walking through a small park she thought about what else had been said. Rather than one argument it had been the continuation of thoughts that had been spoken and not spoken for the last several months, a mix-tape of concerns, complaints and incompatibilities; the latest compilation of their shared lives that had been played at an increasing volume since they had begun to work from home.

What's wrong? He'd ask.

She didn't know ... she felt heavy and weighed down. Nothing seemed to interest her anymore. All days seemed the same. An infinite Sunday. She used to feel sometimes that life was passing her by, but now each day spent looking out of a downstairs window, it was as if life had just stopped. As if she were looking at a still life painting. And tomorrow she would sit, illuminated by her computer's pale light and receive emails that hoped to find her well.

The bleach white lights of the big Tesco, open twenty-four hours, offered some respite from the otherwise grim reality of Sale at night. She walked in the rectangle of light it cast on the floor. Men have it easier, she thought. Everything for them is twenty-four hours. For women it's like late night shopping in a closing shop.

Still Life

She entered, past a young man, wiry with spiked black hair, talking to a young girl, large and bottom heavy in her blue staff trousers and zip up jumper, her hair all kinds of colours. They stood apart and their lower faces were covered. They laughed at something as she walked by. From somewhere above her a song was being played.

Later, she found herself at a self-service checkout, scanning a carton of milk. Green and red lights flashed on and off. A staff member stood to one side in a plastic visor, uninterested and staring at the floor. Disembodied voices spoke to her, asked if she wanted a receipt. Asked if she wanted a receipt. Asked if she wanted ...

Outside, the wind tightened the skin on her face. A man was preparing to get on his bike, fumbling with his bags. He wore grey sweatpants and a brown fleece.

"World's gone mad," he said, as if they knew one another.

She looked at him and raised her eyebrows in recognition. His skin was sallow and stubbled. He sounded like a pack of cigarettes.

"Absolutely mad," he said again, swinging a grey leg over the bike. "Be glad when it's all over, me."

"If it ever is," she said politely, beginning to move away.

"Can't sleep, then? Or's it trouble at home?" he said out of one side of his mouth, cupping a cigarette in his hands and lighting it. The sparks of his lighter illuminated his chin and mouth. Circles of light reflected in his dark eyes.

"Something like that," she looked back, still in motion.

"There's trouble all over," he began to pedal away. "World's gone mad."

She turned to watch his brown figure dissolve into the darkness, losing all sense of shape and form.

Holding the milk in one hand like some pale lantern, she walked down Sale precinct. The streets were empty of people, but littered with their abandoned facemasks. The pubs and bars that punctuated every street corner sat in silence and in darkness, the signage on their windows becoming grimly obsolete.

Unlocked

At the top of the high street a solitary vehicle rounded the corner and rode up the hill over the canal. She followed its path and reached the apex of the bridge, pushing strands of hair behind her ears and then wrapping her arms around herself. Below her the water was black and held patches of moonlight on its surface here and there. It was silent except for the sound of water slapping gently against the sides of narrowboats lined up and down its edges. Some of their windows were orange with lamplight. White smoke rose from one or two of their chimneys. On their walks she'd memorised their names. They'd joked about buying one and sailing away. Or he'd ask her what she'd call hers. Now, they walked in silence or she went alone.

The traffic lights at the crossing burnt orange and then red. It's funny, she thought, how people stop for red lights, even when no one else is around. It had been months since she last drove. Behind her the escalating rush of a tram grew to a crescendo and then stopped below, all beeps and hisses. The carriages were empty. Grey interiors lit up by yellow lights.

She moved on. Shadowy outlines stitched themselves together out of the blue and grey in front of her, but disappeared as she approached. What did she want? How could you ever know? There's too many things and not enough time. Or maybe's there's too much time and not enough things. Days are long. The sun bleeds out. Nights drip.

Without thinking she had returned to their street.

She could sleep in the spare room, she thought walking up the stairs. On the landing she paused and looked into the darkness of their bedroom. What did she want? He'd asked. Right now, to get into bed and fall asleep. She undressed and got in beside him. The world's gone mad and there's trouble all over. Maybe that was true, she thought lying there, but tomorrow the sun would rise, birds would sing, emails would arrive, conversations would be had, hearts would beat and stop beating.

NEW BACKGROUNDS

Chris Nelson

It was, what now passed for, a standard school day. Hannah sat at her laptop waiting for her History class to start. She launched Zoom and adjusted the angle of the screen so that you could see as little of her bedroom as possible. She'd cleared one of the walls of posters and pictures leaving a mostly white background. It wasn't that she was *that* embarrassed about her musical choices, she just didn't want the rest of the class knowing about her current K-Pop obsession. She sighed and checked the clock just as her teacher Mr Barton logged on. Hannah clicked "join" and was suddenly confronted with the usual sea of blinking faces. Pretty much everyone she knew, her entire social world, all bouncing around in their matchbox size frames. Some waving, some pulling funny faces. Class had started.

Sometime later Hannah found her attention wandering. It wasn't as though she didn't care about crop rotation in the fourteenth century – I mean, she didn't, obviously, who did? – it was more that she could see most of her classmates had also started to drift off. Alice Denby was clearly daydreaming out of her window but the arrangement of the frames on Hannah's screen made it look like she was mooning after David Smethurst, which was, frankly, hilarious. Hannah was just about to send Alice a message telling her about this when her eye was caught by a new, tiny pop-up window floating gently, bobbing up and down in the corner of the app. "New Backgrounds", it said, in a soft edged friendly looking font.

Hannah clicked the button underneath the pop-up and was presented with a grid of six shiny new backgrounds to use for the call. Zoom backgrounds weren't exactly banned by the school, different teachers had different attitudes to them, most limited video backgrounds to a standard 'blur' to hide their messy rooms. Mr Barton, Hannah seemed to remember, was fine about most backgrounds, as long as it didn't disrupt the class. Neil Marshall had once uploaded a screengrab from a zombie game his brother was playing. That didn't stay up for long as "Shotguns and RE don't mix", apparently. Hannah started to scroll down the new options. It was, she thought, quite a disappointing selection, there was a beach, the arctic, some ancient ruins somewhere (possibly Greece), the moon, underwater and a jungle. She sighed and clicked on the jungle one. On screen it suddenly seemed that Hannah was sitting in a very realistic jungle. She'd misjudged the software makers, this wasn't disappointing at all. As she watched her picture she could see the leaves on the trees swaying slightly and could even hear, very faintly, the call of tropical birds in the distance.

A chat message pinged in from Alice, "Nice background! Where did you get that?". Hannah replied that it was a new built-in option but it seemed that her software had obviously updated whereas Alice's had not.

"Quit out and re-boot your Zoom?" Hannah sent but it seemed Alice wasn't prepared to disrupt the class just to get a new background.

It was then that Hannah felt something brush past her legs under the desk. She shrieked. Good job that her microphone was on mute. She ducked her head under the desk to see but could spot nothing but wires and a plate with toast crumbs from Sunday. She squinted into the gloom of the desk space but, no, there was nothing there. Meanwhile Mr Barton had spotted her missing from the class.

"Hannah? Hannah, are you still there?" Hannah popped her head up from under the desk to see thirty-one pairs of eyes staring her way. "Yes Mr Barton, sorry, just dropped my pen," she squeaked. Mr Barton nodded sagely and went back to talking about wheat.

It took Hannah several seconds to get over the shock of having something brush past her like that, something warm, something furry, something alive and, as you do, was just about ready to write the whole thing off as something she'd imagined when she happened to notice that there was a monkey sitting on her desk.

Hannah gawped at the monkey. The monkey gazed quizzically back at Hannah. Time seemed to stand still. It wasn't a big monkey, probably about the size of a small cat. Its fur was golden and orange, its feet and hands were pale and tipped with blue. Its face was small and wrinkled but its eyes were black pools that seemed to shine and twinkle with mischief. The monkey seemed quite content to sit on Hannah's desk. Its tail swished a little from side to side while its head tilted and turned as if to see Hannah and her school stationery from every possible angle.

"Hannah! What do you think?" Mr Barton had obviously just asked her a question and judging by his tone, not just the once, but in her befuddled state Hannah wasn't sure whether it was the monkey or her teacher that had spoken.

"Wha ... monkey?" Hannah managed to blurt out which caused the whole class to erupt with laughter. "Monkey? Ms Jones, what have monkeys got to do with rural England in the thirteen-hundreds?" her teacher replied.

Hannah didn't manage to answer him, though, as at that point the monkey, presumably now having taken a good and solid inventory of all of Hannah's stuff chose that moment to grab a pen, one of her good ones, and leap over her shoulder. As quickly as she could, Hannah spun around and the sight that greeted her took her breath away.

Where previously there had been her lovely, if a bit plain, bedroom wall, there was now a jungle. Not a picture of a jungle but a real, living, breathing, moving jungle. Hannah simply stared and stared. This clearly wasn't possible. As she watched she saw water drop from one of the bigger plant leaves onto her bedroom carpet. It fell with a splodge and Hannah could clearly see the dark mark it left there. The sounds of the jungle were louder now too, birds screeched, animals growled and moved through the undergrowth. As she sat, a wind blew through, swishing the leaves and hitting Hannah's face in a warm, damp wave.

The monkey was sitting at the edge, half in the jungle, half in her bedroom playing with the pen. Hannah noticed that the monkey had been chewing one end of the pen and it was possibly this, rather than the fact that her bedroom now seemed to be part of a rainforest, that prompted her into action.

Unlocked

"No!" She shouted, "that pen's part of a set!" and saying that, launched herself from her chair straight at the monkey.

Anyone who's ever watched a nature documentary will know, monkeys are fast. This one, seeing a twelve-year-old girl launching herself at it in a threatening way, didn't hesitate. In a flash the monkey was over the threshold and had gone, disappearing into the jungle with barely a swish. The momentum of Hannah's somewhat rash dive didn't provide her with the same graceful arc as the monkey. She hit the carpet and rolled, in a very ungainly way, over the border and found herself face down with a mouth full of dirt.

Hannah got slowly to her feet and looked around. Now that she was actually standing here, actually standing in the jungle, she became more and more shaken by the reality of the place. The floor underfoot was soft and springy, the leaves that brushed her face were soft and wet. The sounds, smells and the *realness* of the jungle seemed to rob Hannah of any further plans to move. She simply stood, feet apart, her slippers getting soggy, eyes wide, head tilted upwards to the jungle canopy above where she could see beautiful, iridescent birds flying overhead.

Near the top of one of the trees sat the monkey. He looked down at Hannah and she could have sworn that he began to nibble the end of her pen in what seemed like a definite act of defiance.

"Hannah! Are you still there?" Mr Barton, and no doubt the rest of the class, had clearly spotted her absence again. Hannah looked back at her bedroom, at the laptop, at the expectantly waiting class and then turned her head again to look at the monkey sitting triumphantly in the tree.

"Hannah, are you coming back to class?" Mr Barton asked.

As she met its gaze, Hannah became suddenly convinced that the monkey wanted her to chase him. This was a game. She rolled up her sleeves and tensed herself ready to run. The monkey chittered with laughter and Hannah could have sworn that she saw it smile.

New Backgrounds

Without looking back, Hannah said, "Yes sir, sorry, I dropped my pen again. I'm just going to get it back."

History class, it seemed, would have to wait.

LOCKDOWN 2041

Janys Chambers

When I wake up it's winter in my room. There's ice crystals on my window. All I want to do is to burrow down into my huge mound of blankets, but then I hear it. Like a low-down sort of humming, like one of the old lecky machines, only this is a person, not a machine, because it's all stuttery, all broken up into bits with great big choky gasps for air, this is, it's –

"*Mum?*"

She's by the front door, and she's kneeling on the floor holding this bit of paper and hugging herself like she's got a terrible pain. And it's her, it's her making the awful low broken stuttering gaspy sound.

Then suddenly she's on her feet, wiping her face with the sleeve of her old tracky, shouting, "Trace! Trace, get your clothes on, *now*!"

She disappears into the kitchen and starts slamming food and meds and stuff into a No-plastic so fast one of the jars of oatmilk breaks but she just chucks it into the sink and carries on, and it's not like we have rations to spare, is it?

"We can take her some stuff, put it by the gate, she might still be able to – " She stops.

"Who, Mum? What you on about?"

Her mouth twists and her face crumples. She holds out the note.

When we get to Nan's gate, the big red INFECTED – KEEP OUT notice is already on her door and there's a Guard at the gate and of course, she's armed.

Mum walks round the Guard in a big circle and puts down the No-plastic. There's one there already, Uzma-next-door, I guess. I know the bag's been there all night, because there's a thin layer of snow on it. Which means Nan's not been out to get it. Which means –

Mum looks at the house and the blank windows with no-smiley-Nan-face in any of them and then at the snowy bag and then at the Guard.

Lockdown 2041

"Have you seen her at all?"

The Guard looks back at Mum. Mum's face above her mask is all red and wet and it's not just from running here in the cold. I can't see the Guard's face, what with the helmet and the overvisor and the undermask. She might as well have no face. That's a scary thought so I tuck it away under my boots. Nan always says to do that with scary thoughts.

"No. No sign." There's a pause. "Relative?"

"Daughter. And granddaughter."

The Guard nods.

"Okay. You can leave the bag. But no stopping, no vigils."

Mum picks up a lump of frosty tarmac from the road and chucks it hard at Nan's bedroom window. It's a big old lump because all the backroads are rubbish now, with the No-cars. The window cracks. She yells at the top of her voice:

"Mum! Are you there? Can you hear me? It's Yaz, Mum! Please come to the window if you're okay, *are you okay?*"

But Nan doesn't come. The windows look back at us like big blank eyes, and Mum is sobbing now like I haven't seen since Dad, and I don't know what to do, and then suddenly she lunges at the gate and the Guard gets her in a grip, not like, horrible, but, you know, strong, and says,

"Now then, you know you can't go in there."

Mum sort of slithers to the ground. The Guard's still got hold of her and I rush over and grab hold too and under the helmet I can see, now I'm close, the Guard *has* got a face. Eyes. They look quite – kind. The Guard says,

"Look, she might just be asleep. People come through it sometimes, even this new one. Best thing is, go home, keep yourselves safe."

She steps back, suddenly. "Take her home."

We stagger all the way back with Mum weaving about all over the place and I get her into bed and give her the only parats I can find because she's put the rest in Nan's bag and then I sit down.

I think about Nan.

Unlocked

About how she slept on a blow-up by my bed night after night for weeks after Dad. About how she always listens to me chuntering on endlessly about books and random stuff when even Nimmy my bestie sometimes pretends there's something wrong with her audio. About how she loves books too and daffodils and chips, and how much fun it was helping her plant veg in her little Grow-your-own at the back, even sneaking in some daffs she got on the stepmarket.

I know it's up to me. Mum's not really been herself since Dad.

At last, an idea comes.

I haven't used all my Chat today. I type in "Nimmy".

We wait until it's dark, of course. I make sure Mum's in bed, write a note, and creep outside. I haven't seen Nims for months, not since last Lock, and I can hardly see her now because we're both in black with black masks. I think, "She's got taller."

Nimmy says, very quietly, "Sorry she's poorly, Trace."

I act responsibly, I don't hug her, but I think about what she's doing for me, what she's done already – she lives right by the Checkpoint, the risk of it – and tears prickle.

We take backroads, well away from Main-Supply-Drag and the streetlights. We see nobody, nobody breaks curfew any more, get to Nan's corner in twenty. Her house is three along from here so the Guard's very close, I can see the shape of her, sitting on the wall in the dark, very still. I think, "Maybe she's gone to sleep and Nims won't have to do anything." Except then I realise if the Guard was really asleep she'd have fallen off the wall by now. So, she's not asleep.

Nimmy whispers, "Wish me luck."

I say, "Luck."

"And you. Safe."

"Yes. Thank you."

She air-kisses and creeps off down the road at the back of Nan's. A minute later I hear her at the far corner, shouting in her acting voice, "Where am I, where am I?"

The Guard gasps and bounces off the wall like she's been shot and runs to the corner and quick as a flash I run to Nan's gate grabbing

Lockdown 2041

the No-plastics and through. I know she usually keeps her spare keys behind the raincatch, but will they still be there? I even sort of pray as my hand snakes round the tank, and yes, thanks be to No-god, they're there.

I race round to the back door. I hear the Guard shouting "What do you think you're doing?" and "How old are you?" A candle lights in Uzma's window. I can just make out Nimmy's answer in her best bewildered voice, "I think I ... must've been sleep-walking." We did the story of *Macbeth* in Remote Drama.

There's an early daffodil by the step. I snap it off and go inside. The house is freezing. That's the first thing. And dark, that's the second. And silent, that's the worst. Slowly, I grope my way upstairs. Please. Please. Please Nan, be –

Alive. I can see her clearly in the moonlight. She's on her back and her eyes are shut, but she's breathing. It's like, a tiny sort of rasping noise. She has blankets but they're all over the floor.

I tighten my mask and slip some extra ones on top. Five layers. I go up to her. Touch her hand with my gloved one. I can feel the heat even through the glove. I put down the No-plastics and take out a tin of water, cool her forehead, pour a little into her mouth. Some of it dribbles out again but some definitely goes down.

Then I roll her gently onto her front, head to one side. I've seen it done lots of times in films from the old Hospitals before they ran out of staff and shut down, and they always had, like, six people, but Nan's tiny, light as a bird. I might be imagining it, but I think the rasping gets a bit less. I cover her with blankets and stick the daffodil in a bit of water in a vase on her table and look at what else Mum and Uzma packed.

Parats, water, oatmilk, fruit and veg from our Grow-your-owns, some homebake. Enough for a week, and if we can get through that without – if I can keep Nan alive for a week, they'll let a medic in.

I send my love winging through the air to Nimmy, wherever she is, prob'ly still trying to convince the Guard she's really sleep-walked

Unlocked

from her house two miles away to the completely random address of her bestie's sick grandma.

Suddenly, Nan's eyes open. They flicker towards the daffodil, then to me. They change, somehow.

"Yeah, it's Trace. *You're not on your own, Nan.* D'you hear me? I love you. You're going to get better."

The daffodil glows yellow.

FREDDIE THE FIELD MOUSE

Carol Howard

Freddie the field mouse sat in his burrow and gazed at an aqua blue sky.
His mummy had told him he couldn't play out, but he struggled to understand why.
It wasn't too hot, and it wasn't too cold, it wasn't too windy or wet –
As a matter of fact, the day was just right, and that's why he felt so upset.

He hadn't been naughty or wilful or bold, he hadn't been silly or rude.
He'd tidied his toys, he'd finished his chores and he'd eaten up all of his food.
"Oh, Freddie," soothed Mummy, "I know that it's tough, but we both have to do what is best
For the field mice we love, so to keep them all safe we shouldn't go far from our nest."

Trying his hardest to hold on to tears, he quietly nodded his head,
Then Mummy announced with a wave of her leg, "We'll go for a wander instead!
Now wipe off your whiskers and fluff up your fur and tidy your tail with a comb;
I'm sure there are footpaths that we can explore without going too far from home."

Unlocked

Out in the meadow, forget-me-nots swayed, and primroses bobbed in the breeze
While daffodils danced in the afternoon sun and cherry buds bounced on the trees.
"Look at the colours!" gasped Freddie at last, as he took in the wonderful view,
"There's buttercup yellow and bright emerald green and beautiful cornflower blue!"

"We'll make a big rainbow!" his mummy declared, "With petals and clover and grass.
And put it outside as a message of hope to cheer up our friends as they pass."
They foraged for feathers and flowers and ferns, for blossom and berries and bark,
Then laid them together in neat little rows until they'd completed their arc.

"I like making rainbows," chimed Freddie that night, as Mummy picked stalks off his head.
"I'm glad you enjoyed it," she said with a smile, "Now let's get you tucked up in bed."
She popped a big kiss on his velvety cheek and nuzzled his tiny pink nose
Then covered him up with a blanket of moss from the top of his chin to his toes.

Freddie the Field Mouse

The following morning, he woke with the dawn, excited to meet a
 new day.
"Mummy," he bubbled, "the sun's in the sky. Please can I go out to
 play?"
"It's still not allowed," she gently explained, "but why don't I teach
 you to bake
A sweet lemon drizzle, or strawberry tart or a cherry and hazelnut
 cake?"

But Meadow Mouse Market had run out of flour, so Mummy used
 acorns and rye;
She mixed them together then rolled out a crust for an apple and
 blueberry pie.
"Baking is brilliant!" Freddie beamed brightly, his smile stretching
 into a grin
As sugary blueberries burst on his tongue and apple juice rolled
 down his chin.

Days turned to weeks and weeks into months, but still Freddie
 couldn't play out;
He sometimes kept busy with jigsaws and books, but sometimes he
 just lounged about.
"Inside is boring," he wallowed one day, "there's isn't enough room
 to run."
"We'll do a home workout," his mummy replied, "bouncing about
 can be fun!"

Unlocked

They practised their leapfrogs and lunges, and squats, their star
    jumps and burpees and more,
Until they were puffing and panting so hard that they had to lie
    down on the floor.
"That was amazing!" gasped Freddie at last, his heart beating hard in
    his chest,
"I think that I'd like us to do it again, but first I might need a quick
    rest."

Spring turned to Summer and Freddie decided that staying at home
    could be nice,
But then, as the summertime drew to a close, he started to miss other
    mice –
His chums from the meadow, the park and the woods, his friends
    from the playground and pool;
His hundreds of cousins and uncles and aunts, his teacher and
    classmates from school.

And then, without warning, everything changed, and playing outside
    was allowed,
So, Freddie rushed out to the meadow he loved, but it all seemed too
    busy and loud.
Suddenly shy, he longed for his nest and turning to Mummy he said,
"I'd rather make rainbows, or bake a big cake, or do a home workout
    instead."

GEORGE AND THE NUMBER THIRTY-EIGHT BUS

Joy Bryce

George traipsed out of school as usual. The number thirty-eight bus was at the stop as usual, with the engine ticking. He was due home for tea at five as usual. Unusually, George had a new bus timetable in his pocket; he glanced at it before stepping on board and dawdling to his usual seat. It read, school stop: 3:30, then Moscow Red Square: 3:55.

He looked up at the red bus, which was familiar as ever. It had the same décor, seating and dusty windows; nothing unusual there. Even the bell rang as normal. Ding! Ding! They pulled away from the school. George looked to his left through the opaque window and watched as the school receded. The bus took its usual route down through the High Street and out towards the edge of town. George sighed; all was normal, usual and he didn't need to worry.

"Tickets, please!" was the conductor's request. George heard his familiar voice echo from upstairs, and standing up hastily he pulled his ticket from his pocket. The conductor coughed and George turned to find the familiar uniform but worn by a llama.

"Tickets, please!" sounded the voice.

George stared. "How extraordinary indeed," he uttered as the bus trundled on to the next stops, winding its way past all the familiar sights George knew and recognised along the route home. Today, as usual, they would be passing the zoo, George's most favourite place in the whole world: it was truly magnificent. He handed his ticket to the conductor in stunned silence and the llama called, "Next stop, Trafalgar Square."

"Trafalgar Square?" enquired George. "Where are we exactly?" he gulped.

The bus pulled up at its next stop and a well-dressed lion stepped aboard; George couldn't believe his eyes. The creature glanced towards George and then the conductor before sitting quietly by the window. He eyed the notices on the bus and flinched when the bell dinged.

Unlocked

What on earth was going on? George looked round the bus and out of the window; everything else was normal.

George, still on his feet, turned to edge his way out of his seat and towards the lion, but hesitated and then gulped. He sat down again, heavily and uttered quietly to himself, "Should I speak to someone, or ring the bell?"

"Next stop, Red Square!" announced the conductor.

"But we've only just left Trafalgar Square," George declared, unheard by the other passengers. "How can we possibly travel all that way? We can't possibly reach Russia in fifteen minutes, and how does the driver even know the way? This isn't his normal route."

A llama acting as a conductor and a lion in a trilby were quite enough for George for one day and he decided to get off; he would get another bus the rest of the way home. He searched again for the new timetable and looked at his watch; it read: 3:54. "We would normally be where now?" mumbled George.

He looked up and out of the window; in front of him was St Basil's Cathedral, resplendent in the winter snow. The dome of the cathedral was gently covered in snow, patchy and then more even as the snow thickened. It was cold. George gulped again; now this wasn't usual. Neither was the sight of a large bear in spectacles at all normal settling into a seat towards the front of the bus. They had arrived at Moscow Red Square and George had decided to speak up.

"I want to get off!" he squeaked.

"No alighting at this stop!" honked the conductor. "Next stop, Nairobi." George sank back into his seat in disbelief. "But I don't want to go to Nairobi!" he pleaded to the conductor, who appeared not to hear his plea. Ding! Ding! The bell sounded and the bus departed. Frantically, George looked again at the timetable: they were going round the world before tea! The bus drove on.

"Excuse me!" said George. "Excuse me!" he said again, nervously as he leaned forward in his seat. "Isn't this bus going to the terminus?" he asked the lion.

George and the Number Thirty-Eight Bus

"Don't ask me," replied the lion; "I only know where I'm going," and carried on reading his newspaper. "I'm African and rare you know, not as rare as my Asiatic cousins it must be said, but rare enough." Where would they stop next?

George scrambled to his knees on the back seat looking out of the rear window of the bus and stretching before him were the Savannah grasslands of Kenya. The dust from the wheels along the track swirled behind them. "I want to get off!" shouted George. "Stop the bus! I want to get off! Now!" He was silenced by the sight of a giraffe easing itself into a seat, neck low and legs bent to accommodate his height and size. "A giraffe!" shouted George.

"Correct!" answered the animal. "Rothschild, to be precise," added the giraffe.

"Can you help me?" breathed George. "I don't know where we are, or where we are going and Lion can't help, nor Llama. What is going on?"

"Going on?" said the giraffe in a surprised, high pitched tone. "Nothing is going on that isn't usual. We're all catching the bus to the zoo. Hello Lion, I wondered where you'd got to."

"The zoo?" yelled George in a shocked voice. "No, you can't go to the zoo! The actual zoo do you mean?"

"Of course," said the giraffe, putting down a briefcase. "Where else would we be going, given the situation?"

"You can't," said George tearfully. "It's up for sale. The zoo is up for sale. I read all about it in the local newspaper," said George. "It said something about 'insufficient funds' in the article; due to the Coronavirus pandemic, I believe." He reached into his satchel and pulled out several newspaper clippings and proffered them to the astounded creature who stared.

"I know," said George. "I know what we can do, though!" he beamed. George, the giraffe and lion sat together deep in conversation as they hatched a plan. The bus continued on its way, collecting every conceivable rare, threatened, endangered or critically endangered animal and George realised he was witness to something amazing.

Unlocked

They all crowded on the bus and George laughed as he realised, "We've got our own zoo on board the number thirty-eight!"

"My imaginary menagerie," said George. "Except it's real: there's going to be a zoo at my house!" he giggled in excitement with the giraffe and the other creatures. "How good is that?" he declared out loud. How very good indeed: George's very own menagerie.

The day arrived for the big fundraiser at the zoo itself and George was apprehensive but buoyed by the prospect of what could be achieved; today they might just save the zoo and its future existence. Bunting, flags and balloons flew above the zoo to announce the grand opening of the event. The queue was enormous to get in, especially seeing as the zoo had been closed for a few weeks, but now there were more visitors than ever. George and his new menagerie had been doing tours to publicise the event and George, resourceful as ever, had been giving talks in his back garden to raise extra vital cash.

The gates opened and the visitors poured in; every ticket was sold, and donations made in abundance at the entrance, but there was still much to be done. The podium stood in front of him. George coughed, clearing his throat as the crowd fell silent. The only sound was the fluttering of the bunting overhead, even the zoo animals themselves were quiet. He stepped forward; this was it. It was George's big chance. He glanced towards the crowd and caught his mum's eye; she was beaming with pride.

"I have come here today to address you all, not to cajole, plead with or shock you into response, but simply to put to you the facts of the grave conservation challenge we now face. It is one of the utmost severity and urgency; indeed, even in my lifetime I have been witness to tremendous negative change and devastation of not only animals, but the very habitats which support them. For example, as I speak to you all now, the rainforest is being destroyed; every minute acres and acres are being cut down and irreversibly affected. You may well ask, 'What has that got to do with me?' The answer is simple; it has got everything to do with you and your life, for without the rainforests on our planet we are not only denying ourselves the splendour of nature,

George and the Number Thirty-Eight Bus

but disrupting the precarious balance it holds over our existence. Without the rainforests we may be depleted of medicines and even the very air we breathe. Please donate today and save not only these animals, the rainforests but every endangered habitat and animal species under threat, not only our future, but the future of the natural world."

There was momentary silence then George's family rose to their feet, applauding loudly. "Bravo!" shouted his mother, and the crowd agreed; the applause was thunderous. George gasped in relief and delight. "We did it!" declared George to his mum.

"*You* did it, George," said his mum. "And I am so proud of you."

"Can I get the number thirty-eight bus home next week too?" laughed George in triumph.

"What, as usual?" said his mum, laughing loudly.

"As usual," confirmed George with a broad grin. "Nothing unusual on board, I promise."

BEN'S (BORING) LOCKDOWN JOURNAL

Yvonne Oliver-Redfern

DAY ONE
I'm only writing this because a) I'M SO BORED, and b) Mrs T my teacher is making us. On our last school day before lockdown cos of the deadly Coronavirus, Mrs T said we should all make a lockdown journal and maybe we'd put them in a time capsule. I pointed out that we might all be dead, and there might be nobody left to dig it up, but Mrs T said not to be silly – but nobody REALLY knows.

Even if we DO survive, kids of the future will dig it up and find all these diaries full of NOTHING!

DAY FOUR
BORING! I can't see my best friend Freddy, we aren't allowed to go anywhere, and Mum keeps trying to get me to make things out of loo-roll insides and newspaper, or go out in the garden. EVEN WORSE, I have to share a room with my big brother Jay (who's always doing "ninja training" and smells), so Mum and Dad can use mine as an office. They're supposed to take it in turns, unless they have "important calls", but yesterday they squabbled cos Mum says Dad was having an awful lot of "important calls".

My sister Kate says there's going to be loads of divorces in lockdown, that people only realise how annoying each other are when they are stuck together all the time – but I knew Kate was annoying even before lockdown.

She's always grumpy and either stressing about her GCSEs or going on about "huge conglomerates" taking over the world – this really worried me, until she said Amazon (the online shop) was one – I'd imagined something more in the giant slathering monster department.

It's my birthday in four weeks six days, but it's okay – lockdown will be over by then.

Ben's (Boring) Lockdown Journal

DAY SEVEN
Mum and Dad argued AGAIN, this time about him doing his share of schoolwork stuff. He's introduced Games Evening. This sounded fun until I realised all the games involve WORDS, like Boggle and Scrabble. It's just schoolwork in disguise!
    I lost every game.

DAY WHO EVEN CARES?
For some weird reason Mum has decided we must all have dinner together at the table EVERY night, not just weekends. I LIKE eating dinner while watching telly. I don't want to have "meaningful conversation" – what even IS that? Mum keeps introducing "topics of conversation". Tonight, we talked about our lockdown objectives:

> Dad: gardening – yawn.
> Mum: learning to cook properly (be afraid).
> Jay: keep training, so that his ninja skills are in tip-top condition when our neighbours turn on each other for the last loo roll.
> Kate: to save the planet "OBVIOUSLY".
> Me: to survive Lockdown dinners with my family.
> I lost at Scrabble AGAIN.
> At least I have my birthday to look forward to.

DAY NINE
Someone has been pilfering the Kit Kats! We swore an oath not to take more than our ration – one of us is a traitor and I'm going to find out who!
    I'm keeping a close eye on Mum and Dad too. I do NOT want them to get divorced. Freddy's parents are divorced. He can't in lockdown, but normally he swaps between his mum and dad's places and he sometimes gets in trouble for not having his homework or PE kit or something, cos he's left it at the other house. I'm always forgetting things anyway. If my parents get divorced, I'd be in trouble ALL the time.

Unlocked

DAY TWELVE

Unbelievable! The Kit Kat snaffler is Mum! I caught her red-handed nibbling the chocolate from all round the sides.

I had an awful thought and checked the Penguins, and there are only two left even though we agreed we wouldn't even break open the packet till week three. Mum is equally alarmed and takes the stairs two at a time with me racing behind – ten Penguin wrappers are soon discovered in the bin in my ex-room. Dad is the Penguin thief! Kate and Jay hear the kerfuffle and soon we are all shouting.

Later we heard an unfamiliar sound, the front door opening then shutting. After twenty minutes Dad returned from the corner shop with Kit Kats, Penguins, Wagon Wheels, milk and bread. Dad is a hero. He risked his life to get our snacks! The snacks, bread and milk have to stay in the porch for two days, but Mum decides to let Dad in. (Though he has to use hand gel and strip off first.)

DAY SIXTEEN

Mum let me use her phone today to say hi to Freddy. It was good, but kind of weird just talking, we're more the do stuff kinda friends. Last summer we used Freddy's dad's metal detector and found seventeen pence, nine pull tabs, a nail and NEARLY a gun! (Which turned out to be a rusty old garden tap.) He says he's reading lots. (Freddy is weird – he loves books, but it's cool cos he tells me all the stories.) He says I'm lucky cos I have a brother and sister to hang out with, and I say he's lucky because he doesn't.

I wasn't last at Scrabble!

DAY TWENTY

Scientists say kids might be immune from the virus!

Kate says it's Mother Nature punishing adults for wrecking the planet.

Mum and Dad say they don't care if it means we can go back to school.

Ben's (Boring) Lockdown Journal

Jay says if kids take over it will be like the playground when the teachers start chatting – survival of the fittest.

DAY TWENTY-THREE
Our Prime Minister has Covid!
Thousands of people are dying.
I don't want to be an orphan.
DAY DOOM
THREE MORE weeks of Lockdown. Noooooooo – a lockdown birthday!

Mum says getting presents might be tricky, but not to worry, she'll "get creative". Last time that happened I had to wear her home-knitted school jumper with one sleeve longer than the other!

Because of Mum's forty-eight-hour rule I can't have takeaway on my birthday, even though we ALWAYS have takeaway on birthdays. Mum says takeaway left on the porch for two days is probably more deadly than Covid-19, (which is what we all call Coronavirus now – I don't know why). I say at least I'd die happy, but she doesn't care about my happiness.

I won at Boggle!

DAY DOOMIER
Today I saw the heading on Mum's lap top: "Re Covid". Before, I wouldn't have thought anything about it, but now I realised immediately – it spells DIVORCE unscrambled!

DAY THIRTY
Having run out of the pickled onion and salad cream option for sandwiches (a surprise hit), we are down to Marmite, or marmalade found lurking at the back of the fridge.

Mum's suggestion of breaking out the odd tin of corned beef for sandwiches from Jay's "end of the world" hoard obviously made him nervous of looters.

Unlocked

When I try to get in, our bedroom door is wedged shut and has a sign: BEWARE THIEVES WILL BE NINJA'D!

Kate locked herself in her room too, after arguing over whether Mum putting her wet hair in a towel turban was "cultural appropriation"???

Mum and Dad keep disappearing off to the shed (to secretly discuss their divorce?).

I have nowhere of my own to go, so I sit in the garden with our cat Jezebel, the only one who cares.

DAY GAZILLION-BILLION

Five days till my birthday. We can't even get a supermarket delivery slot, so how will they get presents?

Kate and Jay fight about who gets the computer.

Mum and Dad fight about who helps with my schoolwork.

Me and Mum fight about Jezebel. She read cats might carry Covid and thinks Jezebel should stay outside. I suggested Mum should stay outside.

I had a fight with Mum AND Dad about not saying sorry to Mum, and about neither of them wanting me.

I DO want to be an orphan.

(Jezebel is allowed inside though.)

BIRTHDAY EVE

Tonight, was dinner in front of the TV which didn't seem that fun anymore, and no games evening. Mum and Dad went off to the shed for another divorce meeting, probably fighting about who has to have me. I don't want my rubbish birthday. I hope we all get Covid and die!

BEST BIRTHDAY EVER!

No divorce! Mum and Dad were doing up the shed for me. I have my very own place, with a hammock, a chair made of crates and even a bed for Jezebel.

Ben's (Boring) Lockdown Journal

Jay and Kate made my birthday cake, with squirty cream and tinned peaches from Jay's hoard and sparklers for candles.

Mum's cooking practice paid off as the Chinese she made was yummy, and I haven't even opened the pressie waiting in the porch!

We clap for heroes and Freddy and his dad wave from their flat balcony holding a giant sign saying, "Happy Birthday Ben!" They left their metal detector for me to borrow for a while, so I'm going to be busy! Maybe I'll find a time capsule!

HOME-SCHOOLING HERO

Sheila Blackburn

This home-schooling malarkey has left us unimpressed
We won't do exams and SATs, but it's put us to the test –
First up was Maths, and Mum announced, "there's really nothing to it!"
She gave us sums, but all we did was argue how to do it.
I said we should *partition*, using words she'd never known –
That was when she gave me the calculator on her phone!

Mum insisted English was the subject she liked most
She really loved to read and write (but didn't want to boast).
So, Literacy was where we thought we'd really get along –
But then she went and marked all my comprehension wrong.
The Spelling rules and grammar, our Mum just couldn't see
I said: it's SPAG. But she replied, "That's what I'll cook for tea!"

Doing Art was lots of fun and really very messy
Mum declared she needed stuff that wasn't quite so stressy.
My Science tests were not so fair and *doin' in her head*.
"Not a Scientific bone in my body," is what she said.
PE had her doubled in a heap upon the floor
We argued through PSHCE until she yelled, "No more!"

"Computers *are* school work," we said, "it's called IT."
She shook her head and muttered, "hah – you can't fool me!"
Geography and History soon met a similar fate.
The one thing we agreed on – break times were just great.
"This can't go on," cried our poor Mum, looking really glum
"We need something different – our own Curriculum!"

Home-Schooling Hero

And so, week two, we left our books – I learned to cook and bake
Now I know how to peel the spuds and how to make a cake.
Following a recipe helps me read and calculate
And my Eton Mess whips up a scream (and oooh, it tastes just great!).
I have to work out costs and times and measures on my own
But I don't mind, cos these are things I never would have known.

I know how to wrap a present now and how to clean my bike
Find directions with a compass – if I ever need to hike.
I can now sew on a button, use needle and a thread
(I threaded the needle for myself, didn't ask my Mum instead)
It took time and pain and tears from Mum, cos that is what she's like
But in the end, I mastered it – and now I can touch-type!

Week three: First Aid and CPR; we used up all the plasters
Learned to cope in emergencies and all sorts of disasters.
I learned to load the washing machine, set the number on the dial
I even washed the dishes – and that one made Mum smile.
She gave us points on a special chart for all our work and trying
Especially when I made my bed – (I think that she was crying!).

Cleaning shoes and household work got us in a fluster –
Mum hadn't thought what fun you have with a feather duster!
I made up a rota about caring for our pets –
(But cleaning out the rabbit hutch is something to forget).
I bathed the dog and dried him off and even cleaned his ears –
I would have done his haircut, but I couldn't find the shears!

Our *skills for life* timetable is full up to the brim
Now I can now tie my laces and give the hedge a trim,
Or paint a fence, or mow a lawn and I love planting seeds
I can fill a hanging basket and get rid of messy weeds.
Pitching a tent is easy now I can hammer in the pegs –
I've even made a table with some very wobbly legs.

Unlocked

The weeks have come and gone so fast since we last went to school
I miss my mates, of course I do, but these life-long skills are cool.
I've written in my journal, all the things I've learned and done
Thanks to Mum, it's not been bad, cos she has made it fun.
Yes – I know she googled all the stuff and thought she had us fooled
But she's my super hero and I am well home-schooled.

GRANNY FINOLA HAS A SCREAM

Angi Holden

Granny Finola was having a difficult day. Her leg was very sore, even though she had been resting it every day since she fell on the ice. She wasn't able to go for a walk along the lane and say hello to the ponies in the field. She wasn't able to visit the park and feed the ducks and geese. She was fed up of being stuck indoors.

So, she was very pleased when her daughter called round with her grandchildren. Sam and Chloe ran into the lounge and flung their arms around Granny Finola. She gave them both big hugs and told them how happy she was to see them.

"We can't stop long. I need to go to the supermarket," said Mum. "When I told the children I was calling round to see if you were short of anything, they wanted to come too."

Granny Finola picked up her pad and started to write a list. Milk. Bread. Cheese. She thought she could do with some more porridge oats, as she had them for breakfast every morning and the packet was nearly empty. Lastly, she decided that she deserved a treat, so she added a bar of chocolate.

"Right, children, I'll take you back home now," said Mum as she folded up the list to put in her pocket.

"Why don't you leave them with me while you go shopping?' asked Granny Finola. "It will save you a journey and you can pick them up when you drop my things off."

The children thought this was a great idea and pleaded with Mum to agree. She did. Granny Finola sent the children to fetch the box of toys from the hall cupboard.

"Chloe is feeling a bit sad today," whispered Mum. "She's missing school." The children had been off school since before Christmas, and it was a long time since they'd seen their friends, although they had classes online and spoke to them most days.

Unlocked

Sam and Chloe waved goodbye to Mum through the window. Granny Finola had a plan. She asked the children if they would like to paint some pictures. Chloe spread the big plastic cloth over the dining table and got out the paper and pencils while Sam fetched the paints and filled the jam jars with water. Granny Finola shuffled over to the big chair at the end of the table and sat down.

"What are we going to draw?" she asked.

Sam drew the playing field behind his classroom and filled it with boys and girls playing football. Chloe drew the double-decker bus they had passed on the way over in Mum's car. She was two years older than Sam and wanted to draw in every detail of the driver and passengers. It had been nearly empty, but she drew a person in every seat anyway. Granny Finola drew a tree, and a pond with some ducks and geese on it.

"Is that our park?" asked Sam.

"Yes," said Granny Finola. 'I'm missing my walks around the pond." She pointed to the bandage on her knee and pulled a face. "What are you missing, Sam?"

"Swimming," he said. "I'm missing my swimming lessons at the pool." He made big front crawl strokes with his arms, turning his head to the side for a breath between each one.

"What about you, Chloe?" asked Granny Finola.

"My friends," Chloe said, and she began to cry. "I'm missing Sarah and Tom and Becca. I'm even missing Michael, and he's the naughtiest boy in the class!" Granny Finola put her arm around Chloe and gave her a hug, but she hadn't finished.

"I'm missing Mrs Edwards and Miss Murray," she sniffed. "I'm missing English and Maths and History and Science. I'm missing football and netball on the field. And lunchtimes and playtimes. And choir practice and craft club."

Sam offered Chloe the box of tissues and she stopped long enough to wipe her eyes and blow her nose. But still she wasn't finished.

"I miss our head teacher handing out certificates at assembly and visitors coming in to tell us about how things were in the old days.

Granny Finola Has a Scream

I miss going to the library to choose a book for reading practice. I miss school dinners and baking cakes with Mr Jones. I miss Mum dropping us off at the gate in the morning. And I miss looking out of the classroom window at home time and seeing her waiting for us."

"That's a lot of missing and a lot of feeling sad," said Granny Finola. "Do you know what I do when I feel very sad or cross with the world?" The children shook their heads. "I have a little scream."

The children stared at Granny Finola. Their eyes were as wide as saucers. They couldn't imagine Granny Finola having a scream.

"Sometimes I even have a little scream and bang my fists on the table at the same time," she said. "Shall we do that now?"

"Oh no, I don't think that's a good idea," said Chloe. "We might spill the painting water."

"Very wise, Chloe," said Granny Finola. "But we could still have a jolly good scream."

And so that's what they did. They counted to three and then they all threw their heads back and screamed! And when they'd finished screaming, they started laughing and hugging.

"We sounded like wolves," said Sam.

When Mum came back from the shops the children were curled up on the settee with Granny Finola, finishing off a favourite story book. Their paintings were drying on the dining table and their toys lay in heaps on the carpet.

"Gosh, you all look quiet and comfy," said Mum. She looked at the children. "I hope you've been this good all the time I've been at the shops."

"We've been screaming," said Sam. "And making lots of noise!"

"I hope not," Mum said. "Granny Finola is supposed to be resting." Mum looked very worried.

Granny Finola and the children laughed. They explained what they'd been doing. They told Mum how sad they'd been feeling, and how the Very Big Scream had made them feel better.

"I think I could do with some of that," said Mum. "When I was pushing my trolley around the shop a woman suddenly stopped in front of me, and then got cross because I bumped into her. And then I couldn't reach the porridge on the top shelf. And when I went to pay a man was being very rude to the girl on the checkout, even though she was doing her best."

"Would you like a scream, Mum?" asked Chloe.

"I think I would," she said. "Will you help me?"

So, they all counted to three, and threw their heads back and screamed! And when they'd finished screaming, they started laughing and hugging.

"I feel better for that," said Mum.

"You know that any time you feel very sad, or very cross with the world, you can tell Mum how you feel," Granny Finola told the children. "And you can have a little scream together. And a laugh and a hug."

So that's what they did. Whenever they felt very sad or very cross they told Mum and they had a little scream. Sometimes it was only a very little scream, so they didn't wake the neighbours. Sometimes it was so quiet it wouldn't even have woken a mouse. But they always laughed and had a hug together. And they always felt better afterwards.

RESIDUE

Paul Howarth

Switch off the rant and static. Ascend
the stairs in darkness and there, once more spread
your breath across my skin, thin as the pages

that made those fat, heavy books – the ones
that vanished as eager fuel sometime last Tuesday,
yielding only residue and ash. Residue

and ash. Do not question where the Wi-Fi went,
or why, or quite how tight is considered too tight
when it comes to holding

another human being. For dear life. Do not ask
if there is a word for when a continuous sound is only
heard upon its ceasing. The neighbours'

frantic dog was one of those. And now
we've lost our punctuation, our navigation of time
and its passing. And it's passing. Maybe

a vague wall-scratch tally of futile,
forgetful gestures: fingers on light-switches; aborted
offers of tea or stronger; glances

down a hallway, awaiting
a clatter of post that never comes. We have been taught,
and taught very well, to hold

Unlocked

continuity above all, and our bodies
are just refusing to adapt in anything but their own
good time. Maybe that is why you keep

counting spent candles and matches,
tidying empty kitchen cupboards. But please now. Stop now.
Lie a while.

Hold me once more like Pascal's wager,
and ask, what if that was not the apocalypse after all?
What if we were mistaken?

THREE LOCKDOWN DAYS

Jane Thomas

Day 23 – My first visitor

You flew in and were lost
in a world of unreliable air.

Your hardly anything weight
fluffed up, playing with crumbs.

I put you down on the counter
and kept watch and kept watch.

You shook and shuddered
I thought you must be dying.

You looked around nervously
in tiny astonishments and left.

Day 53 – Walk No. 41

Hawthorn drapes hanging
over blushing rose hips.

Bunches of black globes –
sweet, sharp and pip full.

Stains on my fingers and
T-shirt, seeds in my teeth.

The horse hoofed path –
the soft trail to autumn.

Unlocked

A Red Kite circling the last
of the warmth into its wings

wheeling, swooping, mewing
true nature in beak and claw.

Day 103 – The Green Fly

I watch you from the sink.

Sucking on shoots, circling shrubs,
coming to rest on the glazed sill.

Five of your six legs stuck in the gloss,
your nymph feet too leaden to move.

Your autumn wings flapping apace.
Hastening the drying of the paint.

Your teardrop body attracting the gaze
of the orbiting lacewing butterflies.

HOME ALONE

... after Covid-19 has visited and taken away my love

Dick Gilpin

Could be just grey or is it darkest black
Time of loss and sadness; the love I lack!
Greys are darker now than ever before,
The pain of loss leaves me tender and sore.
Home alone is a strangeness and the thought
That this could be the future and we're taught
The basic truth that one of us will die
While one of us will surely have to lie
In the double bed alone. You or I
Will turn over to emptiness, defy
The pains of loneliness and redefine
What life can be as one; and then refine
The mingled strands of thoughts and in that time
Learn how to cope with love passed by and climb
Out of the deep, darkened chasm of loss
And discover once again the new gloss
That covers this dull undercoat of pain,
This incomplete existence, this dread strain
Of being here as me not us; this past
Hope and present nothingness. Will it last
Forever? Does the blankness end? Will friends
Remain as friends or drift away? He sends
A card; they email. Will they still come round?
Were they her friends or ours? What's this I've found
In the cabinet drawer? Like a lost pearl
Of great worth, it sends my mind in a whirl.
A strange day, today – not sure how to say
That this love was and is good ... come what may.

Unlocked

They all sympathise, many do not realise
How loss, emptiness and people who empathise
Bring to me yet more hurtful strain and pain and stress
Where the loneliness is deeper still and will press
Down like a heavy blanket never comforting,
Suffocating attempts to breathe, dislocating
Daily tasks as completely as if guillotined,
squashed, smothered and snuffed out; now eradicated
By some massive blade descending from up above.
Where is now the gentle all-enveloping love
That used to be so calmly taken for granted?
This home alone is the gift I never wanted;
Come back my love, I need you now; your touch would soothe
Bringing hope and light to my life again. Come prove
What we knew together was a treasure house full
Of delights this loss can only blemish and dull.

CHRISTMAS TREE WORMS

Helen Kay

Though the common name prettifies its kind
how grand the Latin – *Spirobranchus giganteus*

and how clever it is, tunnelling tubes
in coral where it can thrive for decades.

Two spruce arms pop out to frisk the brine
for air and food. At the flicker of a light

it slips back safe in its bag, blocks up
the hole with its spiny lid and waits.

The News has arrested my reading;
the virus is mutating; I switch off.

I wrap myself up: gloves, hat, mask,
and drift through the deep December cold,

past a reef of houses – detached, curtains drawn.
I note all the lit trees outdoors this year.

The night is too heavy. I tighten my hood.
Rainbow bulbs pulse: now bright, now dark.

NORTHWICH: FOUR BARE MILES

Kemal Houghton

Strike from the clamour of the town
past the mud-splatter of the cattlefield
         where the Weaver winds away.

Though many wrecks sink into the sea
this one is being sucked into the land.
It is overgrown and sleeps beneath
a winter throw of leaves.

Reeds plug the gap between the quayside
and the river where it decays and falls.
         The river always flows.

This clank and sluice of steel and water
towers on the bank, rises
the boats against nature
         to new heights.

Narrowboats brightly strew a desk
of water; pencils spilt
under a greying sky.
Smoke colours the air
         from a cabin's sleepy stove.

A flash of sun springs from the fields
blinding in the winter mulch
where all growth slumbers
         on the stem.

Northwich: Four Bare Miles

Here Witton Brook is fit to burst;
a dash beneath the bridge
then plunge into the millpond
            uneasing the parked cars.

Now stand the bullocks in their inglorious
mud, with the sound and the smell
of the town in their nostrils,
they chew on time's cud.
No poppies for them
           as they wait
                      in winter's breath

AN INTANGIBLE LOSS

Chris Hollis-Thompson

Someone tried to shake my hand
At once benign, well-mannered, kind
It stirs a strange revulsion now
A sudden pause
Incisive fear
Behind my eyes, new swords are drawn
To clash on virgin battlefields
Risk contends with etiquette
Logic strikes, but habits swerve
Defending the establishment
The human need for social bonds
Physical touch
Something taken for granted until denied then craved like lost love
Surreptitiously divine

The extended palm hangs in the air
Lucid, steeping pressure to oblige
We've shaken before in simpler times
Without the disapproving sentinel of sanitation
So should I succumb to its influence?
Be repulsed?
Aghast?
Or should I retain outmoded behaviours?
Cling to tradition?
Reject the fledgling zeitgeist of this exceptional time
As though the world around us hasn't changed forever

An Intangible Loss

My hesitation broadcasts loud
Teetering on flawed judgement
To choose either extreme seems inhuman
Unnatural
Malignant
So I split the difference
Wrists anchor to thighs, but I make a bold step forwards
Reduce distance to show warmth, though not too close
Then a smile with fixed eyes
No offence
Let's do our part
Our contribution, microscopic yet profound
Like a virus

I cleave our connection with apparent consent
Devoid of outward objection
But you can never tell what others are thinking
What lies beneath that stoic facade
Yearning for lost love
The hand withdraws and emotions sour the silence
Vague melancholy
No smile is returned
Well, they say
Perhaps another time

Unlocked

I nod, of course, and feign agreement
But they can't tell what I'm thinking either
Whether this awkward moment is my latest or first
Whether I acknowledge the changes in the air
Society devolved and then reformed
Links severed, cast aside by sharp misjudgements
The offering of the hand
The pressure to accept
The consequences of rejection
The action and reaction
Shallow acquaintances rebuffed by a self-proclaimed replacement
    "normal"
An intangible, undefinable loss
Leaving so many of us craving lost love

EMBRACING A NEW NORMAL

Joanne Stokes

I'll tell you a story
This is all true
There once was a virus
Much worse than flu
Years ago, when you were small
We were locked down, I do recall
Stay at home, save lives they said
Watching the news filled us with dread
People panicked and stockpiled goods
It would take some time 'til we're out of the woods
Unprecedented was the word
Embracing a new normal, undeterred
We stayed at home and played our part
I tell you this with a heavy heart
Many lives lost to Covid-19
Difficult times, never foreseen
We remember it well, could never forget
To our NHS, we're forever in debt
We only went shopping for our food
A walk or a jog to lift our mood
Now this went on for quite some time
Meeting family was even a crime
We wore these masks to cover our faces
We couldn't go to all these places
Our pubs, the zoo, the shops, the gym
To see them closed was pretty grim
But things got better and we pulled through
Life is a circle that will always renew
We did all this to stop the spread

Unlocked

Thinking of our future and better times ahead
Always be grateful, thankful too
For what you have, who's there for you
We win, we lose, we cherish, we miss
It's always good to reminisce
Live your life with a positive mind
Count your blessings and always be kind
You never know what you might face
But it's always best to just embrace.

SHORTNESS OF BREATH

Matthew Byrne

Shortness of breath, dry mouth, ache in my chest,
Light head, sweaty palms, you know the rest.
Oh how I want to hold your hand,
Severe acute respiratory illness be damned.

No warm embrace, no kiss on the cheek.
Social distancing each time we meet.
Perhaps we could do an alternate greet,
Soul to soul, we can shake with our feet.

Fourteen days, self-isolation,
your sweet lips forbidden temptation.
Dry throat, makes it hard to speak, but
maybe I could see you for a drink in
... about two weeks?

Two metres apart, I long for your touch,
Yet honestly your smile still makes me blush.
Oh how I want to hold you tonight,
We could wear facemasks, seals airtight.

But intimate touch is now deemed uncouth,
Instead I'll preach my love, a gospel truth.
Oh how I want you, here, with me,
Out and about, two lovers running free.

Lockdown rules, but you rule my heart,
It's been that way since the very start.
This time apart can't end too soon,
Romance just ain't the same on Zoom.

Unlocked

Shortness of breath, dry mouth, ache in my chest,
Light head, sweaty palms, you know the rest.
They say these symptoms are probably just a cold,
But you are the one I want to be with, when we are old.

This pandemic soon must pass
But our love could forever last,
A long life together, me and you,
When the Coronavirus is history
like the Spanish flu.

DURING LOCKDOWN

Morgan McIntyre

there is a sharpness   to my bones
where I used to be blunt.
   There is a pale wind
that thrashes through my living room

  and shreds the muted curtains into fibre
that knots my skin and binds me.

One day I will wake without a rising death toll.

One day I will touch my mother's face again.

One day the news will announce our safety
  and people will sit down where they are
and shake
and grab at one another

  arms soft beneath clamped fingers
    wet cheeks pressed to shoulders
pressed to cheeks

  and the jagged empty of my chest
will throb with molten amber –
  a soft ooze of resin
leaking along furrowed limbs
  and thickening
into a frame of honeyed light

as we emerge beneath the breathing sun.

DELAMERE FOREST

George Alldred

The snow, crystalline, pristine, crunches like thunder.
My feet, old but true, fit deep into each print.
Each shape, a palimpsest of my prior self.
I cry, I weep, each tear crashing, deep into the next mould.

The purest flecks of azure dance, waltzing around my weary frame.
I feel the weight of each, the sharpness of their perfect eyes.
Resting their icy points on my skin, piercing and cold.
I plunge my knees into the snow, as I too look to melt away,
    to fade into the night.

I feel the cold as it seeps into the creases of my skin, the fissures of my
    spirit.
My eyes open wearily as I drink in my surroundings.
Like an icy nectar it nourishes me,
Yet, I know that my weak frame contrasts such purity.

At least here, I'm free of confinement, of entrapment, of isolation.
Here, I sing with joyful sparrows
Here, I grow with each branch
Here, my tears are masked by an icy veil; drops upon drops.

Lost in the snow, my sentiments take new dimensions, but lack any
    clarity.
I weep, but for lament or for happiness?
I laugh, but for irony or for joy?
I exist, but for living or for being ... ?

Delamere Forest

I close my eyes, slowly blanketed by a white sheet.
I clench my weakened fist, and feel again
Each nerve, each synapse, each pulse
Here, lost in the Delamere frost, I remember that I am living.

DEAR STRANGERS

Dana Roberts

The other day across the road I spotted a stranger
His headphones on, singing as he walked
So unbothered and immersed in his world
I smiled at this simple joy, then felt a pang of sadness
A world now so dominated by warnings and reminders
To keep your distance, create that space
A space so physical, but maybe more than that?
Days spent deciding to steer myself into traffic
Rather than getting too close to an elderly couple
Worrying I came across rude when I smiled at the cashier
Because how would they know?
We are so used to finding joy in the company of strangers
I long for a drunk woman to compliment my dress in a club toilet
To have an elderly man sit beside me on the bus
And tell me how much the city has changed
I even want to go in for a hug when they wanted a handshake
My only sliver of social contact with strangers I craved
In the form of reassuring others I wasn't in the queue
Tentatively taking my coffee from the hands of a barista
The occasional weather talk with strangers in the street
To persuade others I'm still socially competent
Smiling at the stranger and his headphones
I realised I missed those strangers
With this social barrier keeping us apart
And I was tired of my four walls and the same faces
I remember seeing a man playing guitar on the street at night
And shamelessly singing along with a group of strangers
I remember countless overcrowded train journeys
Forced to sit on the floor by the doors
Mutual eye rolls and small talk with passengers

Dear Strangers

Christmas light switch-ons and concerts
Apologising for standing on someone's foot
Catching someone's eye singing the same words as you
And trying not to let go of my friend's hand in the crowd
The stranger with headphones made me think
How happy we are in the company of a happy stranger
Life had suddenly got very serious
Every interaction risk assessed and distant
Though not all is lost in the two-metre space between us
Right now we may not be able to do a lot of things
But we can make conversation at the bus stop
We can compliment someone's mask in the supermarket queue
We can ask the cashier how their day was
We can appreciate a stranger singing with his headphones on
So I will keep my distance but only with the pavement between us
Because I miss you strangers and the times we had
I'll see you again soon

REMEMBER THAT TIME?

Zoë Lambrakis

(we will say)
Remember those days?
When breathing the same air as your loved ones
Was a danger to your life.

Remember the long months
When we all stayed inside
Crossing off the endless days.
The novelty,
The boredom.

And underneath it all the fear.
We gave a wide berth to strangers.

Remember that?

Calculating the distance
Between us.

Before everything shut down, that was.
All the familiar things.

Our whole way of life, really.
Funny to think of that now.

Remember those things we took for granted?

The touch of another living soul.
The warmth of a human body
Other than your own.

Remember That Time?

The memory of a thudding heartbeat
Enclosed in a tight embrace.

It couldn't be more different
The then and the now.
Could it?

And we will laugh
Roll our eyes a little
As we try to brush off those memories.

Though I feel your hand grip mine
Just a little bit tighter now
As our fingers intertwine.

HOME SWEET HOME

Caitlin Norbury

1. EXT. REID HOUSE – AFTERNOON
It's another grim, rainy day. We're outside a small two-up two-down. The paint on the brick wall has peeled off over long, wet years and the wheelie bins outside the door look ready to spew.

In the distance, we hear the incessant barking of a neighbour's dog.

The only colour that stands out comes from a piece of paper stuck on the downstairs window – a messy rainbow is painted on the page and in smudged letters:

"THANK YOU NHS".

2. INT. REID HOUSE – SAM'S BEDROOM – AFTERNOON
The bedroom is small and cluttered with toys, superhero posters and videogames. We hear loud EXPLOSIONS and GUNFIRE from the TV speakers.

Slumped on the bed is SAM (twelve). He's the kid teachers moan about in the staff room, the boy with the face that spells:

T-R-O-U-B-L-E.

His unblinking eyes are hard with concentration as he aggressively jabs the buttons of a PS4 CONTROLLER. Sam never takes his eyes from the TV screen, even when –

His mother, TANYA (thirty), enters and gathers in one arm the debris of dirty laundry strewn across the floor. Judging from her roots and fading tan, she's barely coping under lockdown rules.

Home Sweet Home

TANYA
I bet you've finished your schoolwork
if you're playing that, then?

SAM
(bluntly)
Yeah.

Tanya gives Sam a knowing look, she wasn't born yesterday. She grabs the school WORKBOOK from the floor and flips through it.

TANYA
(assertive)
You've not even started! Right, get this crap off.

Sam flippantly glances up at Tanya and continues playing his game.

SAM
I need to finish this round –

TANYA
Now.

Tanya walks over to the TV and turns it OFF. Sam is riled and begins to whine –

SAM
Mum!

TANYA
You can finish your work downstairs.
I told you before, Sam, I'll take the
PlayStation out your room if I can't
trust you to –

SAM
(moodily)
Fine!

Unlocked

Tanya smiles down at her son and holds out her hand as a peace offering. He rolls his eyes and, refusing the hand up, stands up from the bed.

TANYA
(friendly)
Come on, mardy bum.

Tanya follows Sam out of the room.

TANYA
And stop being cheeky!

3. INT. REID HOUSE – LIVING ROOM – AFTERNOON

Despite the effort to make the small space homely, the room more closely resembles a doll's house cramped with oversized furniture.

EVIE (six), a boisterous little girl with clothes stained with food and paint, noisily plays with her toys on the floor.

Sam and Tanya sit together on the couch. His schoolwork is open on his lap, but he is distracted by the TV.

BBC News is playing. A WOMAN is being interviewed on her doorstep by a male REPORTER, who stands a safe distance away from the woman.

WOMAN
My dad died alone in hospital – and there
was nothing we could do to help him …
That's something we'll never *ever* get over.

Sam surprises himself as his eyes well up with TEARS when the woman on the TV fails to choke back sobs. He uneasily glances over at his mum, who stares at the TV absentmindedly and chews on her nails … she seems anxious, but Sam is too busy violently rubbing at his eyes to stop unwelcome tears from falling.

Home Sweet Home

Tanya is startled when her PHONE rings and she springs up from the couch, forcing a big bright smile.

> TANYA
> (to Sam)
> Hun, I need to take this call for a bit.
> Keep an eye on your sister and
> I'll let you play on your game tonight.

Tanya reaches out to stroke Sam's hair, but he whacks her hand away as though it were infected with deadly germs.

> SAM
> Promise?

Tanya is already halfway out the room.

> TANYA
> Promise.
> (into phone)
> Hello?

Beat.

> Yes, this is Tanya Reid.

Sam watches Tanya leave the room and turns his attention back to the TV.

> REPORTER
> Is there anything you would
> like to say to the viewers at home?

> WOMAN
> Our family have lost so much this
> weekend ... but I know we're not the only ones.
> We're all in this together so please –
> *please* stay indoors and keep
> yourselves and your loved ones safe.

Unlocked

Sam sighs. He looks down at his WORKBOOK and begins writing.

4. INT. REID HOUSE – LIVING ROOM – LATER

The open workbook now lies on the couch beside Sam, half-finished and forgotten. He has changed the TV station and is watching CARTOONS. Evie sits on the floor, now staring up at the TV with open-mouthed wonder.

>   EVIE
>   (still staring at the TV)
>   Sam ... It's teatime. Where's mummy?

>   SAM
>   I already told you, she's on the phone.

>   EVIE
>   But that was *ages* ago.

Pause.

>   I'm hungry ...

>   SAM
>   (frustrated)
>   Can't you wait a bit?

Evie shakes her head.

>   SAM
>   Fine ... I'll ask mum. Don't. Move.

5. INT. REID HOUSE – KITCHEN – MOMENTS LATER
Sam appears in the doorway –

>   SAM
>   Mum?

He glances inside the room and leaves.

Home Sweet Home

6. INT. REID HOUSE – UPSTAIRS LANDING – MOMENTS LATER

Sam reaches the top of the stairs and walks to TANYA'S BEDROOM. He leans in through the open door –

>   SAM
> Mum, you in here?

Empty silence. He stands in the doorway of his mother's bedroom for a moment, a puzzled look on his face. It's like the house just swallowed her up.

Then we hear a hushed voice through the closed door of the BATHROOM. Sam edges toward it slowly. He stops outside the bathroom door and listens ...

>   TANYA (o.c.)
>   (upset)
> Yes, I know my rights – I have none.

Beat.

> No, I already told you – I only worked there
> a year so they don't owe me redundancy
> pay or nothing.

Sam's eyebrows furrow, trying to work out what's being discussed, judging from Tanya's tone he knows it's nothing good.

>   TANYA
> I just – I don't know what I'm gonna do now,
> Mum ... I'm already falling behind on bills
> as it is and –

Tanya's voice breaks and she begins to quietly cry.

>   TANYA (o.c.)
> I just feel like I've failed the kids.

                           Unlocked

Sam hovers outside the closed door as realisation dawns on him. He suddenly feels uncomfortable eavesdropping and takes a quiet step back from the door –

                          EVIE (o.c.)
                            (loudly)
                     What are you doing?

Sam is startled out of his bubble and sees Evie standing at the top of the stairs. He quietly rushes over to Evie.

                             SAM
                          (whispers)
                       Go downstairs.

                             EVIE
                            (loudly)
            Why are you whispering? Where's mummy?

We hear the toilet FLUSH from the bathroom. Sam looks terrified as he tries to hurry Evie down the stairs – but she won't budge.

Tanya steps out of the bathroom with a carefree smile, but her eyes, still raw with tears, betray her.

                            TANYA
                What are you two troublemakers up to?

Evie pushes passed Sam and skips over to Tanya. She cuddles her legs and looks up at her mother with an excited grin –

                             EVIE
                     Mummy! What's for tea?

                            TANYA
                 I should have known! Greedy guts!

Home Sweet Home

Evie laughs and Sam watches his mother's exaggerated happiness with quiet apprehension. Tanya lifts Evie up into her arms.

> TANYA
> Come on then, dustbin.

Tanya heads down the stairs with Evie in her arms. Sam stands awkwardly at the top of the stairs, unsure what to do with himself. Then Tanya calls up –

> TANYA (o.c.)
> You coming down?

7. INT. REID HOUSE – KITCHEN – EVENING

Sam and Evie are sat at the kitchen table. The radio is playing some upbeat song and Tanya is singing along as she bustles about with pots and pans.

She places TWO PLATES of fish fingers, chips and beans in front of Evie and Sam. Without a second to spare, Evie starts digging into her meal, but Sam can't bring himself to eat. He watches Tanya open the backdoor and light a cigarette.

> SAM
> (quietly)
> Aren't you eating anything?

> TANYA
> Nah. I'm not hungry.

Sam looks down at his meal.

> SAM
> Do you want one of my fish fingers?

> TANYA
> No ta, love.

Unlocked

> SAM
> Go on. Have one. I'm not that hungry either.

Tanya frowns at Sam and glances at the two fish fingers on his plate.

> TANYA
> Are you sick or something?

> SAM

Beat.

> No?

> TANYA
> Something wrong with my cooking?

> SAM
> No.

> TANYA
> Right. Then get it down your neck.

Tanya gives Sam an authoritative stare, waiting for him to start eating. Sam looks defeated as he forks a chip into his mouth.

> TANYA
> (satisfied)
> You're a growing boy so eat your food.

Tanya looks over at Evie, who is steadfastly demolishing her meal and has bean sauce everywhere.

> TANYA
> Maybe Evie can teach you a thing or two.

We look down at Sam's plate as he slowly eats his meal ...

DISSOLVE

8. INT. REID HOUSE – KITCHEN – LATER

Sam forks up the final chip into his mouth. Tanya takes the plate away and carries it to the sink to be washed. It's just the two of them now, Evie has been tucked in for the night.

Despite the noisy washing of pots and happy pop tunes on the radio, there is a tense silence that hangs in the air like a balloon ready to burst.

> TANYA
> If you've finished your schoolwork
> you can play on your game before bed.

Sam's expression isn't too thrilled. He fidgets, trying to express what's been playing on his mind, but gives up and stands from his chair.

> SAM
> Okay.

When he leaves the room, Tanya drops a pot into the soapy water and hunches over the sink, deflated.

9. INT. REID HOUSE – SAM'S BEDROOM – LATER

Sam has returned to his original position: slumped on the bed with console controller in hand. But something has changed, he isn't jabbing the buttons passionately but with an apathetic slowness.

The game makes a sound effect:

"GAME OVER"

Sam drops the controller down on the bed beside him.

He sighs and looks around his room at all the things his mother bought him over the years. His gaze dulls with guilt.

Unlocked

Then his eyes fall onto a superhero poster. The character stares ahead with pride and power. A woman clings onto the superhero with a serene expression. She's safe in his arms.

Sam's eyes brighten at the image and he sits up with renewed resolve. He darts to the chest and opens a drawer. He roots through it until he finds what he's looking for ...

10. INT. REID HOUSE – TANYA'S BEDROOM – NIGHT

Tanya's room is bare compared to Sam's bedroom, too basic and plain to be considered homely. It's dark inside the room and the only light shines through the doorway from the landing.

Sam is standing by the bed and in his hands is a PURSE. He zips it closed and is placing it in a bright red HANDBAG when suddenly the room is flooded with light. The ceiling light has been switched ON.

Sam jumps with fright and turns to see Tanya stood in the doorway. She spots the purse in his hands and her face contorts with fury. In a useless attempt to save the situation, he quickly drops the purse back into the handbag.

> TANYA
> What the bloody hell are you doing?

Tanya's voice is booming. Sam is frozen as though he had looked into the eyes of Medusa.

> TANYA
> Well?

As she waits for Sam to answer, Tanya notices her reflection in the mirror. She sees her face deformed with anger and her expression softens with shame ...

Home Sweet Home

            TANYA
            (sighs)
Look, I know it's been hard on you – not
being able to see your mates ... being stuck
with me and your sister every day ... But I
can't have you acting up right now.

            SAM
I didn't –

            TANYA
            (snappy)
Don't!

            (calmer)
Don't interrupt me when I'm speaking ...
You're not the only one who's having
a hard time – so grow up and stop being
so selfish.

Sam furrows his eyebrows angrily and his face scrunches up as he tries to find the words to express his emotions, but he gives up and shouts –

            SAM
I hate you!

He pushes past Tanya and runs out of the room. Tanya stands gobsmacked as she watches Sam disappear. Unsure of how to respond, she yells back –

            TANYA
Get to bed!

A lonely silence follows and Tanya slumps down onto the bed, burying her head into her hands in defeat.

Unlocked

11. INT. REID HOUSE – SAM'S BEDROOM – NIGHT

The room is dark now, other than an orange glow that soaks through the curtains from the streetlamps outside. Sam lies in his bed, wide awake, staring at the ceiling.

The door quietly creaks open and Tanya pops her head inside. Sam quickly turns on his side and pretends to be asleep. Tanya steps in and closes the door quietly behind her.

> TANYA
> I know you're not asleep.

Sam doesn't reply.

> TANYA
> I'm turning the light on.

She switches the light ON and perches on the edge of the bed.

> TANYA
> (playfully)
> I found fifty pounds in my purse ...
> I think it might be magic.

Beat.

> TANYA
> (seriously)
> I'm sorry for earlier, okay? And thank you, but I can't accept it.

Sam suddenly sits up –

> SAM
> What? *Why?*

Home Sweet Home

> TANYA
> I don't know what you heard today
> but you don't have to worry about a thing.
> I'll sort it.

> SAM
> But I want to help! Just keep it!

> TANYA
> It's your birthday money, Sam. You should
> be spending it on something fun.

> SAM
> There's nothing I want to buy.

Tanya places the cash on Sam's bedside table.

> TANYA
> Then put it somewhere safe
> until you see something you like.

> SAM
> Why won't you let me help?

> TANYA
> I don't need your help, love. All I
> need you to do is focus on school
> and stay out of trouble.

Tanya smiles, soft and sincere.

> TANYA
> I love you so much. I honestly don't
> know what I'd do without you.

Sam still looks dejected and Tanya strokes his hair softly. He doesn't push her hand away this time.

Unlocked

> **TANYA**
> Things are gonna be a bit uneasy for a while, but money problems come and go. What matters is that we're together. So keep your chin up, kid, okay?

> **SAM**
> Okay ...

> **TANYA**
> Promise?

Sam's gaze finally meets Tanya's and he smiles.

> **SAM**
> Promise.

> **TANYA**
> It's late. Get to sleep.

She stands.

> Night, love.

Tanya walks over to the door and Sam sinks down into the quilt. She reaches out for the light switch –

> **SAM**
> Mum?

She looks over to Sam, who is now lying in bed facing the wall.

> **SAM**
> I love you.

> **TANYA**
> Love you too.

Beat.

Home Sweet Home

SAM
Are we gonna be all right?

A smile forms on Tanya's lips, but her eyes betray an uncertainty ... She opens her mouth to answer –

CUT TO BLACK

I AM STARS

Julie McKiernan

Jasmine, seventeen+, who has a learning disability, sits very deliberately and carefully on a chair.

JASMINE

Mum say sit here. Sit here and wait.

Pause.

I am sit here. But mum go out. Mum go to work. Corona say she has to. But Dad must stay home. Mum say Dad will get big fat bottom. Dad say Mum already have one. Mum smack Dad! Jo-Jo laugh. We all laugh!

She laughs then, determined.

Dad say sit here and wait. Dad go out. With Alfie.

Mimics her dad's voice.

"Stay there, Jasmine. You can take Alfie out later with Jo-Jo."

Sighs.

Jo-Jo say –

Mimics her sister's teenage voice.

"Go away Jas. I'm FaceTiming Ben. Go and wait downstairs." I am downstairs.

Beat.

I am waiting.

I Am Stars

Looks around. Thinks.

> I am waiting for minibus but Corona say no minibus. Mum say minibus having rest from noise.

Beat.

> Beep beep BEEP!

She imitates the female transport support staff, loud voice.

> "True Colours taxi! Morning Jasmine, rise and shine, need to get to work on time. Look lively now." Morning, Mrs Davies. Morning, David.

Action.

> Rock rock. Morning Billy.

Raises hand to slap his in greeting.

> Morning Tom.

Fist in air.

> Ci-ty! Morning Kirstie.

Mimics Kirstie with fast speech.

> "Did-you-watch-*Coronation-Street*?-I-watched-*Coronation-Street*-I-like-*Coronation-Street*."

Thinks.

> I am waiting for *Emmerdale*. Every night. Dad say *Emmerdale* rubbish but me, Mum and Jo-Jo like *Emmerdale*. Cafe is open. Shop is open. Pub is open. In *Emmerdale*. Corona shut True Colours. Mum say –

Mimics Mum's affectionate voice.

Unlocked

      "Wendy had no choice darling. She had to shut down." But Wendy say –

Mimics Wendy.

      "Bye bye, Jasmine. See you Monday."

Firmly.

      Monday is Shopping and Crafts.

Concerned.

      My Easter bunny only got one ear. We squish tissue paper and stick it –

Demonstrates.

      down. Jo-Jo say it will be Christmas bunny now. Jo-Jo is stupid. Corona is stupid!

Sulkily, building.

      No True Colours. No swimming. No shopping. No dancing. No rugby. No cinema. No cafe. No Maccie Ds! I hate Corona!

Stands in frustration and bites her hand. She paces then stops.

      Dad say –

Mimics her dad's voice.

      "It's only for a few weeks, Jasmine. It'll be over before you know it."

Agitated.

      But I know it! I know it! It not fair! Corona not let Jasmine see Nan.

Mimics her nan's voice.

I Am Stars

"How's my lovely girl? Give me a big squeeze."
No squeezes. No kisses. No cherry scones – no
Grampy! Grampy say I am his sunshine. Tuesday,
Grampy wait for Jasmine outside True Colours.
Grampy's car stink of fish. Pooo! Grampy shouts –

Mimics her grampy's voice.

"Fish ahoy! Get the pan on, woman!" Nan gives
Jasmine fish fingers.

Beat.

Tuesday is Art and Gardening –

Stops, concerned.

My turn to water vegetables! Who will water
vegetables? Corona will kill vegetables! Corona
kill people –

This is too much to process. She stands and paces to reassure herself.

I-am-waiting-for-Wednesday. Music and
Cooking. Me and Kirstie make cupcakes!

Excited.

Wendy say lick spoon but Kirstie get on nose so
I rub all over face!

Demonstrates.

Kirstie scream and hit me with spoon and put
icing in hair! Daniel laugh.

She stops, shy and sits back down.

Mum say sit here. Sit here and wait. For nice
surprise.

Unlocked

Thinks.

    I am waiting for summer holiday. In Devon.

Getting excited.

    In cottage. With beach. And ice-cream. And funfair and horses going up and down.

Demonstrates.

    Nan and Gramps play cards and Jo-Jo goes –

Mimics her sister's teenage voice.

    "I'm bored."
    Ben is boring. He want to –

Makes exaggerated kissing face and sound.

    All the time. Dad say –

Mimics her dad's voice.

    "Give it a rest, you two."
    But Jo-Jo say –

Mimics her sister's teenage voice.

    "That's what boyfriends do, Jas."
    No they don't!

Beat.

    Don't have to!

Beat, firm.

    Boyfriends help you and be kind.

Thinks.

I Am Stars

> I am waiting for Thursday. Health and Hygiene.
> Wendy paint my nails with white sparkle and
> Daniel say they look like stars. I have stars on
> fingers! In relaxation time Wendy read story
> and we move our hands. My stars twinkle.

Thinks.

> Dad say –

Mimics her dad's voice.

> "Look at the stars, Jasmine. They know when this
> will end." I look but they don't say. Mum say I
> talk too much. Not listen! Mum tickle me!

Beat.

> I love mum. Don't want her to go out. Corona
> might get her –

She starts to panic, remembers then puts her hands together in her lap and closes her eyes.

> Nan say –

Mimics her nan's voice.

> "Breathe. It'll only happen if you let it."

She breathes deeply for a few moments then opens her eyes. Shyly.

> I let Daniel hold my hand!

She places her hands over her mouth in shock then takes them away and smiles. She confides.

> In PE. We play parachute game. Up and down.
> Up and down. Then run under. We sit under.

Unlocked

> Outside. Eat sandwiches. Daniel held my hand and I let him have sandwich. After, our hair went – whooooo!

She demonstrates the effect of static on hair.

> Wendy say we look like dandelions!

She blows as if on a dandelion clock.

> But Daniel say –

Imitates Daniel's romantic voice.

> "You are stars."

She is suddenly very shy.

> I tell Jo-Jo. But she laugh. She say –

Mimics her sister's teenage voice.

> "OMG. I'd barf if Ben said that. He'll be asking you to marry him next!"

She stands, agitated.

> Corona stop Daniel ask! Corona stop Jasmine see Daniel!

Beat.

> Mum say sit here and wait. Dad say sit here and wait. Jo-Jo say wait downstairs but Jasmine say: Want Daniel!

She paces frantically then abruptly exits. Offstage we hear a scream of frustration followed by banging and muffled conversation. After a few moments she re-enters looking scared. She drops to the floor, curls up into a ball and rocks.

I Am Stars

>Door is locked. Door is locked! Jasmine bang but Jo-Jo say –

Mimics her sister's teenage voice.

>"It's for your own good, Jas. Dad told me to lock you in."

Tearful.

>Why?! Why Jo-Jo lock door? Why Dad tell her?

Frets. Thinks. Alarmed.

>Corona trying to get in! Corona come for Jasmine and Jo-Jo!

Thinks.

>Mum out there! Dad out there! Alfie out there! Corona out there!

Panic. She bites her hand.

>What we do? What we do?

She starts to panic, remembers, then squeezes her hands together and closes her eyes.

>Nan say –

Mimics her nan's voice.

>"Breathe. It'll only happen if you let it."

She breathes deeply for a few moments then suddenly opens her eyes. Gasps. Works through the problem.

>Jo-Jo not let Corona in. Jo-Jo lock door. Dad say wait. Go out with Alfie. Mum say wait. Nice surprise. Alfie is good dog. Alfie is big dog.

Unlocked

> Alfie kill Corona! Alfie kill Corona and all go out! Jasmine go True Colours, see Daniel, see Nan and Grampy! Yay!

She dances excitedly then stops abruptly. Thinks. She returns to her chair.

> I am downstairs. I am sit. I am wait.

Pause. Sighs. Pause. Suddenly she notices something through the window.

> Dad!

She jumps up and waves.

> And Alfie! Brave Alfie!

Waves with even more enthusiasm then stops, puzzled.

> Why Dad pointing?

She moves towards the window.

> Who is coming?

She looks across the road.

> Man. Woman –

Beat, surprised delight.

> Daniel!

She waves with great enthusiasm.

> Daniel! See me! I am Jasmine. I am lovely girl! I am stars.

GAME TIME

Roberto Rodriguez

FADE IN.

INT. A PHONE VIDEO CALL – EARLY MORNING.

It's 1:51 am. We see a split screen. JOSH, sixteen, baby-faced, is sat at his desk in his bedroom, looking down at his phone, which is propped up next to his computer screen, the only illumination in the room. MAISY, sixteen, tall, slim, sits up in her bed, holding her phone. She turns on her bedside lamp.

                    MAISY
Jesus, Josh, it's nearly two, why are you calling?

                    JOSH
It's an emergency.

                    MAISY
What, God, are you sick or something?

                    JOSH
No, I'm fine, sound as a pound.

                    MAISY
Are you joking? You've woken me up for nothing?

                    JOSH
Not nothing, but something, something big and super-sick. I've just found a game that's saying it'll give you money every time you level-up, I shit you not.

Beat.

Unlocked

MAISY
What are you talking about? Have you literally gone insane?

JOSH
The only insane thing is this game, Maize, honest to blog, it's called *Panacea* and it's our golden ticket, I know it.

Josh adjusts his phone so his computer screen is more clearly in shot.

MAISY
Okay, fine, where are you? Let's start with that.

JOSH
Games Kong, a new, magic thread on the Dark Web.

MAISY
Are you kidding me, the Dark Web? After *everything* you said about not going on it again?

JOSH
Look, *don't* believe the muggle media, it's not some evil place full of paedos and drug dealers.

MAISY
But you *swore*.

JOSH
Maize, I swear a *lot*.

MAISY
Josh –

JOSH
Okay, fine, I *did* promise, but then I regrew my balls and changed my mind, and you will too when I tell you about this game. It's offering hundreds of thousands of squid for completing it, Maize, it's already given me fifty squid

Game Time

in Bitcoins just for finding it, but I have to answer three questions to access the game proper. *That's* why I belled you up, I need your help.

MAISY
Jesus, are you even listening to yourself? Sorry, so let me recap, you've just found a game on the Dark Web that's offering thousands of pounds in prize money, and what, you're *not* immediately thinking this is Scam City? Why would a game just *give* you money?

JOSH
Ah, well, this is the good part, the sneaky as fuck part, see, it's not like every other game, where you can play as long as you want, no, you have to *earn* game time by streaming yourself carrying out dares. The more crazy the dare, the more game time you earn.

Beat.

MAISY
Sorry?

JOSH
I know, fucked-up, yeah? The thing is, if you complete Level One, you win a thousand squid, if you complete Level Two, you get another two grand, it doubles every time. If you get to the end, you win just over half-a-mill. Think about it, Maize, that's *serious* coin. My dad's lost his job because of this Covid-19 shit, so has your mum, just imagine if this pans out and we absolutely smash it, we'd be rich.

MAISY
No, Josh, come on, this is just –

Unlocked

JOSH
Total bullocks? Yeah, it might be, I get that, but we don't know till we try, do we? And anyway, like I said, it's already given me fifty big ones, so it doesn't just talk the talk, it walks the walk.

MAISY
It's just reeling you in, Josh, God, can't you see? Seriously, just log out, go to bed and get some sleep, you've been stuck indoors too long, you're not thinking straight –

JOSH
(sharply)
No, Maize, I'm thinking clearly, for maybe the first time ever. I've got to step up. Dad's banging on all day about bills, he's saying we might have to start using the food bank again, we might even lose the flat, he's necking more and more Prozac and sleeping pills, that's the only reason I can play games all night, because after eight, he's virtually dead, this could be our way out. I'm doing this, Maize, with or without you.

Josh glances at his computer screen.

Shit, she's coming back.

MAISY
Who?

JOSH
Weirdo Woman, Lori Reversing, she's like the host, she said she'd be back with three super-hard questions.

Josh readjusts his phone and tilts his computer screen so Maisy can get a clearer view of the screen, which displays lines of text which fade away and are replaced by a floating female head.

Game Time

Can you see her?

MAISY

Yeah, just.

Maisy squints and sees on Josh's computer screen a silver-skinned woman with a blonde beehive haircut and red glasses with lenses shaped like five-pointed stars.

JOSH

Maize, you *gotta* help us answer these questions, if this *is* kosher, we can play together and split the money, but we *only* get one shot. If you get a question wrong the game freezes you out for a week until you can try again.

MAISY

But this is just –

JOSH
(very intensely)

Please, Maize. Things are just shit here now all the time, my dad's like a zombie, I've not seen mum in weeks, we need a way out, I need a way out.

Beat.

Please, Maisy. For me.

Josh's fingers twitch and sweat slicks his forehead.

MAISY
(quietly)

Okay.

Josh smiles, relief flooding his face.

JOSH

Great. Thanks, Maize. You're the best –

Unlocked

> **LORI**
> (on the computer screen)
> So if you've read the Terms and Conditions, we can proceed. Remember, you have only thirty seconds to answer each question. Ready?

> **JOSH**
> Okay, thinking boots on –

> **LORI**
> Question One. The quick brown fox jumps over the lazy dog, is an example of a ... what?

Lori disappears and is replaced on Josh's computer screen by the question she just posed, written in large black text. A blinking cursor flashes up in the top-left-hand corner of the computer screen, and a timer appears in the top-right-hand corner, counting down from thirty.

> **JOSH**
> It's okay, I'll google it.

Josh swirls and clicks his mouse.

> **MAISY**
> The quick brown fox jumps over the lazy dog –

> **JOSH**
> (manically tapping the mouse)
> Shit, it's not letting me bring up another window.

> **MAISY**
> It's okay, I've got it, it's a sentence which contains all the letters of the alphabet. A ... palindrome.

Josh puts his fingers on the keyboard.

Game Time

No, no, it's pangram, *not* palindrome. It's pangram, I think.

JOSH

You *think*?

MAISY

No, I'm sure, it's pangram.

Josh types "pangram" and presses Return. His computer screen goes black.

JOSH

It *was* palindrome. Always go with your first –

There's a loud PING! and a greenish-blue tick with a black head scuttles across his computer screen. Lori reappears and grins.

LORI

Correct.

Josh lets out a big breath.

JOSH

Never doubted you for a second, Maize.

The blinking cursor and timer reappear. The timer has reset to thirty.

LORI

Question Two. Name this Cheshire village, often home to TV stars and Premiership footballers.

Lori dissolves into a large thumb, which comes down violently and crushes a strawberry at the bottom of the computer screen.

JOSH

Cheshire, shit, we virtually live in Cheshire, we must know this –

Unlocked

MAISY
I can't see it properly, Josh, you're going to have to describe it.

JOSH
Okay, it's a big thumb coming down and crushing this ... strawberry or raspberry, at the bottom of the screen.

Josh readjusts his phone and computer screen.

No, it's a strawberry, defo, and the thumb's coming down and squashing it over and over.

Maisy stares at her phone.

Fifteen gone –

MAISY
I got it. Prestbury.

Josh looks at her blankly.

My mum worked there at one of the restaurants when I was small, The Bridge. It's Prestbury, I'm sure.

Josh looks back at his computer screen as the thumb comes down again to crush the strawberry.

It's a strawberry, or *berry*, being *pressed*, see? Pressed berry ... Prestbury.

Josh types "Prestbury" and presses Return. The computer screen goes black. There's a loud PING! and another tick scuttles across the computer screen. Lori reappears and grins.

LORI
Correct.

Game Time

                JOSH
Nice one, Maize ... and thank God your mum didn't decide to go on Jobseeker's.

The blinking cursor and timer reappear, which has reset to thirty.

                LORI
Now for the third and final question. I am the beginning of everything, and the end of everywhere. I am the beginning of eternity, and the end of time and space. What am I?

Lori disappears and is replaced on Josh's computer screen by the question she just posed, written in large black text.

                JOSH
Did you hear that? I'm the beginning of everything, and the end of everywhere. I'm the beginning of eternity, and the end of time and space.

                MAISY
It's too long to google in time.

The seconds tick past with Maisy deep in thought.

                JOSH
Come on, this is the last one, we're nearly there.

                MAISY
I'm thinking, I'm thinking.

Josh glances at his computer screen, and back at his phone.

                JOSH
Fifteen gone.

                MAISY
It's love.

Unlocked

Josh puts his finger on his keyboard's L.

> No, it's God, it's God.

Josh looks at Maisy.

> JOSH
> Which one is it?

> MAISY
> It's God, I'm positive.

Josh types "God" and looks at the screen, reading the question again.

> Josh, press Return.

> JOSH
> No, it's *not* God, I think it's E.

> MAISY
> E? What, ecstasy? Jesus, you're always thinking about drugs –

> JOSH
> No, I mean the letter E.

Josh deletes "God", presses E and Return as the timer hits zero and a buzzer rings. The screen goes black. Josh kicks his desk leg.

> JOSH
> Fuck ... too la –

Catherine wheels explode across the top of Josh's computer screen. Lori's grinning face reappears at the bottom.

> LORI
> Congratulations. You were successful.

Maisy smiles and Josh fist-pumps the air.

Game Time

>JOSH
>Get in –

>LORI
>Welcome to *Panacea*.

Lori disappears from Josh's computer screen and is replaced by a flashing phrase:

GAME TIME!!!

    GAME TIME!!!

        GAME TIME!!!

Josh grins and looks back down at his phone.

>JOSH
>We did it, Paisan, we *actually* did it.

>MAISY
>We did, thanks to you.

Josh makes a fist with his right hand, extends his fist towards his phone screen, then stops.

>JOSH
>Shit, I forgot.

He unclenches his hand, curls up his right arm and presses his elbow against his phone's screen. Maisy smiles and does the same and they "bump elbows".

>I am *literally* convelling. I tell you, I've not felt this good since I got Pinocchio to put his nose up my arse and made him tell lies.

Unlocked

> MAISY
> Anal sex jokes now, Josh? Seriously?

Josh smirks and looks back at his computer screen, which now shows a panoramic view of the inky black of space as it slowly creates planets, stars, asteroids, moons and twin suns.

> JOSH
> God, the game's like ... forming a new universe, Weirdo Woman said each one was personalised. It's double-pukka.

> MAISY
> Seriously, though, Josh, coming back to planet Earth for a sec, I repeat, have you thought about *any* of this? *Properly*, I mean?

> JOSH
> Yeah, loads.

He looks back at Maisy.

> I thought about it properly when I was scan-reading the T & Cs, I was thinking about it properly when I called you, and I'm thinking about it properly now –

> MAISY
> But again, why would a game give you cash for levelling-up? How could it even *afford* to do that, if the game's free?

> JOSH
> It could make that cash back with in-game purchases, Maize, *Fortnite* and *Pokémon GO* made billions, and let's be honest, it'll probably be *so* rock, no-one will even complete Level One, never mind the whole thing, but it's like I said, we won't know till we try, will we? Come on, you can't tell me you weren't into it when you were

absolutely smashing that quiz like some sort of Stephen Fry with baps.

MAISY
(sharply)
I was in the moment, Josh, I was ... in the zone. It was my fault for letting myself be sucked in, but this ... dares thing is *really* scary. It's *beyond* sus, it's like *Blue Whale* or something.

JOSH
Come on, if it gets too dark or intense, I'll Gareth Bale, simple as. And if it *does* turn out to be a big marketing scam from some new publisher, say, trying to make his game stand out, and there's *no* dares and *no* more money, so what? At least I'll get to play a cool new game and kill some time while we're all grounded.

MAISY
But why would a publisher even drop their new game during a pandemic? And why did we not even hear about this ... *Panacea* till now?

JOSH
Because some spatulas are actually *good* at keeping secrets, Maize, specially when their jobs depend on it. And dropping it in the middle of a pandemic's genius, seeing as most of the planet's at home and bored out of their skulls, and gaming more than ever, and exploring the Dark Web more than ever. Imagine if it's got loot boxes and shit, and millions of people play, they'll make their money back in weeks, days even.

Beat.

See, I *have* thought about it, youth.

Unlocked

There's the faint sound of a door being opened and soft, padding footsteps. Maisy looks off-screen and lowers her voice.

MAISY
That's my mum, I'm going to have to go, if she comes in and sees me talking to you she'll kill me.

JOSH
Okay.

MAISY
I'll speak to you in the morning, we'll talk about this a *lot* more then.

JOSH
Okay, until then. And thanks again, Maize, for everything. Seriously, I couldn't have got through these last few months without you. There's no one else I can talk to twenty-four/seven, or who puts up with me being such a stressed-out fucknugget all the time.

Maisy smiles.

MAISY
No problem. See you later.

Maisy puts her phone on her bedside table and turns off her lamp. Josh looks back at his computer screen. Lori reappears, floating above a universe now filled with purple planets, and stars and asteroids and green moons and shimmering twin suns.

LORI
Once again, welcome to *Panacea*, a new kind of game for a new generation of players. Remember, the first thirty minutes of play is free, given as a reward for successfully answering our fiendish quiz, but each subsequent minute of time must be earned.

Game Time

                JOSH
            (very brightly)
This is *on*, Joshy boy ... this is on like *Donkey Kong* playing ping-pong with his dong –

                LORI
Okay, space cadet, a new world awaits. Happy exploring, and good luck.

The computer screen's universe dissolves into a bright, shining white. Josh grabs his mouse and smiles.

                JOSH
    Game time.

He glances at his phone and notices that Maisy hasn't hung up. He reaches down and terminates the call. The screen goes black.

SMALL TALK

Tim Elgood

Short radio play

Nanna's big day was never going to be a breeze for Poppa. Socialising can be a stormy affair. Knowing what to say on restricted-size family occasions is sometimes best left to smaller people.

Characters

POPPA (aged seventy-one) Reserved by nature.

RUBY (aged ten) Disinhibited by nurture.

Echoing interior of large communal room. Indistinct polite group chatter is heard amidst the faint backdrop of tape-recorded music from the early 1970s. Joni Mitchell is singing "A Case of You" (1971).

       RUBY
Poppa?

       POPPA
Here we go.

       RUBY
What?

       POPPA
Bet you've come over here to tell me what to do.

       RUBY
How are you?

Small Talk

POPPA

Fine.

RUBY

Sure?

POPPA

Why wouldn't I be?

RUBY

How do you think it's going?

POPPA

Far too slowly.

RUBY

Shouldn't you be "circulating"?

POPPA

I knew you'd come over to tell me what to do.

RUBY

I asked you a question, Poppa.

POPPA

Which was?

RUBY

Shouldn't you be circulating?

POPPA

Pauses to sip his drink.

Quite possibly.

RUBY

So are you *going* to be circulating?

Unlocked

POPPA

Sips his drink again.

Quite possibly not.

RUBY

What is "circulating"?

POPPA
A form of torture.

RUBY
Well Mum thinks you ought to go and do a bit of it.

POPPA
Well you go back and tell Mum I'll leave that delight to her.

Sips his drink.

And while you're there you can add that I can do without ...

RUBY
Your ten and a half year old grandchild telling you what to do.

POPPA
Something along those lines.

Beat.

RUBY
Do you reckon there's going to be enough buffet?

POPPA
I have grave doubts ... excuse the pun –

Small Talk

RUBY
We queue like that at school for dinners.

POPPA
... grieving seems to make our extended family extremely hungry.

RUBY
Great Uncle Jim told Dad that he and Great Auntie Jackie couldn't eat their hotel breakfast because they both felt too upset.

POPPA
In that case the buffet will very soon be history.

Sips his drink.

RUBY
They don't look like they very often skip breakfast.

POPPA
They're not called "Great" Uncle and "Great" Auntie for nothing.

RUBY
They said they were glad you organised a proper "gathering" for Nanna now lockdown's over.

POPPA
Nanna's having a posthumous send-off.

RUBY
What is "posthumous" ... is it a "dip" like taramasalata?

POPPA
It was certainly a dip in form for Nanna.

Unlocked

RUBY
Mum was saying we must expect you to struggle a bit today.

POPPA
I'm glad she shared that with you.

RUBY
She didn't ... she just didn't realise I was sat on the next loo. She was shouting out to Great Auntie Emma who was using the hand dryer. You should get something to eat while there's still some left ... we don't want you drinking on an empty stomach.

POPPA
God ... you sound like Nanna.

RUBY
Don't say "God", Poppa ... especially not today.

POPPA
Why? Do you think he'll hold it against Nanna? Refuse her entry into heaven on the grounds that she might still have Covid?

RUBY
You might not believe in heaven ... but some of us do.

POPPA
Like who?

RUBY
Me and Archie Conway to start with.

POPPA
Not Archie Conway who rarely gets to the school toilet on time for his wee?

Small Talk

          RUBY
Doesn't stop Archie believing in heaven.

          POPPA
Each to their own.

          RUBY
You often have to rush to get to the toilet on time for your wee.

          POPPA
It hasn't turned me to God ... quite the opposite.

Finishes his drink.

I'm off to get a refill.

          RUBY
I'm off to get you a plate of food.

          POPPA
You'll do no such thing ... I'm not hungry.

          RUBY
You can't just drink red wine all afternoon ... you'll be "fit for nothing".

          POPPA
I swear it could be Nanna speaking.

          RUBY
It was ..."If the worst happens, Ruby ... be sure to keep an eye on him on my big day ... else he'll be fit for nothing."

Cut briefly to music. Neil Young sings "Old Man" (1972). FADE BACK TO DIALOGUE.

Unlocked

POPPA
I'm never going to eat all that.

RUBY
What about a "thank you, Ruby"?

POPPA
Thank you, Ruby.

RUBY
I saw you making a bit of polite conversation at the bar ... good boy.

POPPA
I used to leave the small talk to Nanna.

RUBY
What is "small talk"?

POPPA
Stating the obvious ... through a mouthful of finger buffet. It was always best left to Nanna.

RUBY
You can't leave it to Nanna today, Poppa.

POPPA
Thank you for pointing that out, Ruby.

RUBY
It was Nanna who pointed it out ... she told me to remind you to be on your best behaviour. She also said to make sure you eat something ... So come on ... "chop chop".

POPPA
I never believed in reincarnation before today.

Small Talk

RUBY
She said I would need to be your "right hand girl" today.

POPPA
When did she say all this?

RUBY
Before she went to hospital ... when I told her over the phone that I had decided to do my school project all about her ... about when she was young and everything. You shouldn't have put that whole scotch egg in at once.

POPPA
(speaking with difficulty)
It was *half* a scotch egg.

RUBY
Honestly (!) ... that's how snakes eat ... chew it up properly, please.

POPPA
(with mouth still full)
So ... go on.

RUBY
Where was I?

POPPA
Talking with Nanna over the phone gossiping away about your school project.

RUBY
Well it wasn't "gossip", really ... not "small talk" ... it was proper grown up big talk. Except she was a bit breathless with her asthma.

Unlocked

POPPA
What did she tell you?

RUBY
All sorts.

POPPA
Like what?

RUBY
Like how some people find it difficult to express their emotions when things get serious and sad.

POPPA
Were these "people" sometimes husbands and grandfathers and things like that?

RUBY
Loads of people don't like talking about death, Poppa. I didn't talk for most of an afternoon when Frodo my hamster got eaten by next door's cat. Now have that sausage roll ... but bite it in half ... don't just bung it in.

POPPA
(eating)
So carry on ... what else was said?

RUBY
Well ... Mrs Woolacott said that although you are a man of few words –

POPPA
Hang about ... who's Mrs Woolacott?

RUBY
You know Mrs Woolacott.

Small Talk

POPPA
Do I?

RUBY
You've met her at the school gates ... my form teacher.

POPPA
Oh her ... so what did she have to say on the matter?

RUBY
Mrs Woolacott said that just because some people don't always want to *say* how they are feeling doesn't mean that they don't *have* feelings.

POPPA
Was that it?

RUBY
No ... what Archie Conway *really* loved most was that it was Nanna who had to give *you* the first kiss in 1971 because you were so shy and ...

POPPA
Okay ... press "pause" ... just ... remind me how Archie Conway has got in on this debate?

RUBY
Well not just Archie Conway ... my whole class ... they all laughed out loud ... when I read my project out. The bit about you first meeting at the music festival and you with shoulder length hair and no bald patch.

POPPA
Bald patches weren't in fashion.

Unlocked

RUBY
Anyway, Mrs Woolacott asked everybody to settle back down and that gave me the chance to tell them all how worried we were about you.

POPPA
"We"?

RUBY
Me ... and Mum and Dad ... once Nanna had gone into hospital. And Nanna of course ... she was terribly worried about what might happen to you. Now eat something else ... don't just play with your food.

POPPA
Let's put food on the backburner for a minute.

RUBY
When Mum read my school project she couldn't stop crying and Dad had to say "there, there" and cuddle her.

POPPA
And where were you?

RUBY
Sat at the top of the stairs ... it was night time. Then she stopped crying and Dad made a cup of tea and they both sat and talked about you.

POPPA
Me?

RUBY
Yes ... and wondering if it wouldn't have been better if it had been you who'd gone first.

Small Talk

POPPA
It's beginning to cross my mind.

RUBY
I'm going to make sure you "cope" Poppa and that you don't become a "liability" and I'll teach you to make small talk to other people because you and I make loads of small talk don't we? Don't worry ... I'm going to be your "right hand girl".

The background recorded music is turned off and tapping upon a microphone is heard.

POPPA
(over microphone)
Er ... can you all hear me?

The hubbub subsides to a stone silence.

"Unaccustomed as I am" ... et cetera, et cetera ... You probably weren't expecting a few words from this "man of few words" today ... But ... wonders never cease.

Polite group laughter.

I must own up that the "few words" aren't mine ... they are those of my right hand girl stood alongside me here. So without further ado ...

Sound of paper being unfolded. He reads apprehensively.

"It was very wet and muddy at the festival and ... he was rather shy and quiet ... and I was rather loud and drunk ... but do you know something? Even then I thought to myself ... this is the one for me."

Unlocked

FADE IN MUSIC AS SPEECH FADES OUT. James Taylor, "You've Got a Friend" (1971).

> " Well ... if I'd waited for him to kiss me, Ruby, I'd still be waiting today ... so I did no more than lean in and ... "

MUSIC PLAYS OUT

ROSE WALKER

Simon James

ANNA
(exasperated)
Okay ... let's do a couple more and then we can all go for a much-deserved lunch break. Why don't we look at another subtraction? They *are* a bit trickier, but more and more of you are starting to smash them now. Tamika. *Tamika.* Remember Tamika, even though you're sat at home, I can still see you if you've got your camera on. That's it – if there's something up your nose, go and get a tissue.

Sighs.

Okay. All right, let's try this one. It's tricky because it's a subtraction ...

Speaks slowly while writing on a whiteboard.

One and three-quarters ... minus two-thirds.
Now, remember what you've got to do: make the denominator the same for each fraction, so you know what you're working with. Michael, you need to put the iPad down now and start working this out on your pen and paper. Okay Year Six, if you think you have the answer, put your hand up. Eira, what have you got?

Beat.

I think you're on mute, Eira.

Beat.

Still on mute, Eira.

Beat.

Unlocked

Okay, I've read Eira's lips, and I'm pretty sure she said one and one-twelfth. We had to convert it into twelfths, so ...
(writing)
... one and nine-twelfths minus ... eight-twelfths is ... one and one-twelfth.
(lost the will to live)
Okay, go and have your lunch, be back here at one.

The Zoom call "pings" to an end. The laptop is closed with a heavy sigh. Anna walks downstairs.

SAM
How's it going?

ANNA
(dejected)
It's going.

SAM
That bad?

ANNA
It's like they're different people when they're at home, honestly.

SAM
Would you say this is cooked?

Beat.

ANNA
It certainly was five minutes ago.

SAM
Get some plates out, then. Different people how?

Rose Walker

ANNA
At school they're in an environment *designed* for learning, so they all just crack on with what they've got to do. At home ... they're *trying*, bless them, but it's obviously so hard for them to concentrate on what the teacher is saying when she's in a little box on a screen and they can hear their Xbox whispering to them from next door. *I* can almost hear it!

SAM
Babe, if you're starting to hear voices, maybe we should book you in to see someone. Over Zoom, obviously.

ANNA
And so many of them are sat in the same room as their parents who I just *know* are scrutinising everything I say ... I can actually see some in the background watching! How off-putting is that??

SAM
Oh God, don't check the news then.

Knives and forks chinking.

ANNA
(eating now)
Why?

SAM
Your mate Gav'la Education Seccers has just said if parents aren't happy with their teachers they should report them to Ofsted.

Beat.

ANNA
Well, that was nice of him, wasn't it?

Unlocked

SAM
How is it? Not too burned?

ANNA
It's all right. Listen, *I do appreciate you making my lunch while I'm teaching* –

SAM
(pointed)
Good.

ANNA
... But it does ... *interest* me that you manage to go through three pans making one omelette.

SAM
I couldn't find the jug.

ANNA
(swallows food)
What's that right there?

SAM
Oh yeah.

Beat.

ANNA
I've got a favour to ask you.

SAM
This is on top of me being your personal chef, yes?

ANNA
You know how we do Star of the Week?

SAM
You teach astronomy?

Rose Walker

ANNA
I've let this week's winner, Olivia, choose whatever she wanted as a prize.

SAM
That's ballsy of you, giving a ten-year-old free rein.

ANNA
Well I said it couldn't cost me actual money.

SAM
Good, the old joint account has taken a bit of a battering this week.

ANNA
You remember when I told them you were a famous guitarist?

SAM
(wary)
Yes ... As a joke because they were being too nosy ...

ANNA
Yeah, well it's kind of turned into a thing and they all think you actually are one. Anyway ...

SAM
Presumably "financial risk analyst" isn't sexy enough for the primary school audience, then.

ANNA
Okay, side note: never use the word "sexy" when we're talking about primary school children, okay?

SAM
Understood.

Unlocked

ANNA
So basically Olivia asked if she could have a Zoom call with you and I said yes.

SAM
With *me*? Sorry, what?

ANNA
It's fine.

SAM
Is it?

ANNA
She's one of my five nice children. She'll go easy on you.

SAM
Well that's very good of her. Is she Chip Shop or Pony Club?

ANNA
Kind of in the middle. And don't you dare let slip that that's what we call them.

SAM
What does she want to talk to me for?

ANNA
So she can brag to the others that she met you, probably. Just get the guitar out, play her "Smoke on the Water" ... you'll be done in five minutes.

SAM
I *do know* other songs you know.

ANNA
Course you do, love.

Rose Walker

SAM
It doesn't sound like I have any say in this?

ANNA
I'll make it worth your while tonight ...

SAM
Careful, this is still a discussion involving primary school children!

ANNA
I was talking about a lasagne. What were *you* talking about?

Music. Transition to next scene.

OLIVIA
Hi!

Beat.

I can see you but you're on mute.

SAM
Oh yes, sorry. Hello Olivia! I'm Mr Walker.

OLIVIA
I thought you two weren't married?

SAM
Erm ...

OLIVIA
I know your surname is Jones, *and* I know you're not actually a famous guitarist. I googled you.

SAM
Oh, okay.

Beat.

Unlocked

I can still play "Smoke on" – I'll put this away.

    OLIVIA
Can Miss Walker hear me?

    SAM
No ...

    OLIVIA
Can I see the rest of the room, please?

    SAM
I'm sorry?

    OLIVIA
Just turn your laptop around so I can see she's not there.

Shuffling around. Laptop being moved.

    SAM
I feel like I'm being investigated!

    OLIVIA
And behind the screen, please.

    SAM
That's a wall ...
    (disgruntled)
See?

    OLIVIA
Thanks, sorry. I like your coffee table.

    SAM
Thanks, Anna picked it.
 (realising he's slipped up – panic)
Sorry, I mean Miss Walker –

Rose Walker

OLIVIA
Don't worry, we all know her name is Anna.

SAM
You do?

OLIVIA
It's on her badge. All right, so, what's her favourite flower?

SAM
Who, Anna?
    (realising he's done it again)
Miss Walker?

OLIVIA
    (duh)
Yes.

SAM
Er ... I've no idea.

OLIVIA
What!? Come off it! You live together! How can you not know what her favourite flower is??

SAM
Because! We're a busy couple! We don't have time for –
    (aside – more to himself)
Oh, wait – I think I *do* know.

OLIVIA
Yes?

SAM
I'm pretty sure it's a rose. That was her grandma's name and ... yeah, I'm ninety per cent sure it's a rose. I can check with her?

Unlocked

OLIVIA
Nope, let's go with that. How big's your garden?

SAM
Here I'll just show you, you've seen the rest of the bloody house.
    (panic at the swear word)
Sorry, I mean – seen the rest of –

OLIVIA
Yeah, yeah.

SAM
Can you see that?

OLIVIA
Yeah, that's great, thanks.

SAM
What are you writing down?

OLIVIA
Don't worry about it. Are you working from home on Tuesday?

SAM
Why?

OLIVIA
(duh)
Well that's the day she goes in to teach the key worker kids, isn't it?

SAM
So?

Rose Walker

> **OLIVIA**
> If I were you, I'd make sure you get lots done on Monday ...

> **SAM**
> What, why?

"Ping". Call ends.

> Olivia?

Beat.

> Bloody hell.

Beat.

> Definitely Pony Club.

Music. Transition to next scene.

> **SAM**
> (on phone)
> Yeah, no – all good. Well, just like half the country I guess – spending most of my time sat in my kitchen slaving over my laptop. And by "slaving over" I mean waking up one-minute-before-work-starts and shuffling through the day at the absolute slowest pace that I can, sending tactical emails at the right times so my colleagues think I'm busy.

Beat.

> Yeah, pretty much. I mean I'm meant to be working *now*, but you know.

Beat.

> No, don't worry, that's what I'm saying, it's a lot more chilled out.

Beat.

> Yep, totally. My favourite is when you're on a Zoom and you've got a –

Beat.

Unlocked

Zoom. Erm do you remember Skype? It's just the latest name for video calling. But yeah my favourite is when you're on a Zoom and you've got a fart brewing, so you mute yourself, fart, and then unmute yourself, all within the space of a couple of seconds.

Beat.

No Nana, because if I went next door, they would *see* me get up and leave.

Beat.

Because it's rude – you're meant to be in a meeting!

Beat.

(exasperated)
No, obviously I wouldn't fart in an actual meeting, I'm just saying: this is one of the only upsides of doing it remotely.

Beat.

It *is*, actually. The skill is in the speed: click-fart-click, dead fast so no one notices, and you've got to be careful you don't give the game away with your face.
(responding to sarcasm)
No, that's *not* what they taught me at uni, but if I was studying there *now* it's definitely a skill I'd be picking up quick …

Beat.

Yeah, she's all right, thanks. You know. Obviously I wouldn't say this to her face, but she's *definitely* busier than me.

Beat.

Yep, but then she goes in on a Tuesday to teach the kids of the key workers.

Beat.

Well you *say* that but you'd be surprised – her school have had over a hundred kids sent in. I don't think the government have been as strict this time with which

Rose Walker

parents get a free pass to palm off their –
(seeing something, observing to himself)
What's this guy doing?
(into phone)
Nana, can I ring you back? This bloke's started unloading his van on my drive. All right, thanks.

Hurried moving – to outside. We can hear cars.
(raised)
Can I help you, mate?

DRIVER
Just unloading this delivery.

SAM
What delivery?

DRIVER
(straining)
Thiiis delivery.

SAM
Woah. I think there's been a mistake.

DRIVER
Says they're for Anna Walker, number seventeen? Here's the note.

Paper rustle.

SAM
(reading)
"Dear Miss Walker, we wanted to let you know – "

Beat.

Oh, bloody hell.

DRIVER
That's the lot, anyway.

Unlocked

> **SAM**
> I would hope *so*! Look, I don't think I can accept these, mate ... what am I meant to do with them all?

> **DRIVER**
> Dunno, pal, but the delivery instructions say "leave on the drive if no one in" – so I couldn't load them back up even if I *wanted* to.

> **SAM**
> That's ridiculous. So you're saying I could pay you to go and dump whatever I wanted on the drive of someone I don't like?

> **DRIVER**
> (completely ignoring him)
> Let me just take a little –

Camera snap.

> Cool. All right, that's me. I can't take them back, but I *can* offer a word of advice ...

> **SAM**
> Oh yeah?

> **DRIVER**
> I'd dig out a pair of marigolds if I were you ... Have fun!

Sam sighs heavily. Music – transition to next scene. Door opens.

> **SAM**
> Hey.

Rose Walker

> ANNA
> (ardent)
> Sam, where did all those bushes come from? Are they ours??

> SAM
> Well they're planted in *our* garden ...

> ANNA
> Oh my God. They're gorgeous. Are they *rose bushes*??

> SAM
> They are indeed.

> ANNA
> You remembered?? About my gran?

> SAM
> Well kind of. No, I mean, I absolutely did. But don't shower me in gratitude just yet; they're not from me.

> ANNA
> Then who – ?

> SAM
> Have a read of this. It came with them.

Paper moving.

> ANNA
> "Dear Miss Walker. We wanted to let you know how much we appreciate ... "
> (welling up)
> " ... everything you've ... " Oh I'm too emotional to even read this!

> SAM
> Pass it here, read it in a bit.

Unlocked

Paper moving.

> **ANNA**
> Give me the top line.

> **SAM**
> Olivia's dad works at a garden centre, but they've completely closed, so Olivia thought it would be a nice idea to give you some of their stock.
> (cynically)
> I mean, they still weren't free – they've made *that* crystal clear – five of the kids' families clubbed together. Presumably your five nice ones.

> **ANNA**
> I'm – I don't even know what to – thank God they're not here, I'd be sobbing all over their jumpers!

> **SAM**
> Famously illegal.

> **ANNA**
> That's so, so lovely of them.

> **SAM**
> Yeah. I mean, they weren't lovely enough to actually come and help put the things in the *ground* ...

> **ANNA**
> Who planted them?

> **SAM**
> Obviously you haven't seen these fingernails yet. I should have told her you liked daffodils.

Rose Walker

ANNA
You planted them? What about work?

SAM
Finally! Someone remembers that I have a job too!

ANNA
It must have taken you all day. Have you got loads to catch up on tonight?

SAM

Beat.

Nah, I boxed it all off in an hour, but still.

Beat.

I'd like credit for not lying to you then, please, and the same amount of appreciation I would have gotten if I *did* have to work late.

ANNA
Okay, lovely one, one appreciative lasagne is heading your way tonight.

End music starts to play, increasing in volume.

SAM
Chances of that one being a euphemism?

ANNA
Pretty slim; this conversation was very child-heavy.

SAM
I feel like my whole life's child-heavy at the moment.

Unlocked

ANNA
You had a five-minute Zoom call with *one* kid. Why don't you try teaching long division to thirty of them at once when two of them can't take their eyes off the TV, another one's picking her nose –

Music has now engulfed the dialogue.

END

This play was dedicated to Miss Williams.
I don't know how you do it. x

YOUR COURAGE, YOUR CHEERFULNESS, YOUR RESOLUTION WILL BRING US VICTORY

Ben Saunders

FADE IN
INT. LOCATION #1/ – NIGHT
Modern high-rise apartment block with floor to ceiling glass windows which don't open and without a balcony, giving a feeling of luxury but also compact to develop sense of confinement.

CHARACTER #1: CATE
Young female character sat on bed, moves towards floor to ceiling windows of apartment block, sighs and places hands against glass looking out into the night, and pauses pressing head against the glass looking trapped. In the background a smart speaker is on with a BBC Radio 4 show.

>SMART SPEAKER
> An earth-like planet has been discovered forty light years away from our own and has been named LHS 1140b. The planet orbits a red dwarf and is believed to be the best chance of having advanced life forms as it is in what is known as the Goldilocks zone between …

> CATE
> Turn radio off.

Silence. She checks time on phone and throws it onto her king-sized bed. The computer makes a high-pitched series of beeps, she goes over to the oversized computer screen and accesses computer conferencing (e.g. Zoom). She clicks a few times and a large face appears on the screen (of CHARACTER #2).

> CATE
> So good to see your face. Even like this.

Unlocked

CHARACTER #2: TOM appears on screen only in the browser window.

TOM
Yeah babe, how did it come to this? I can't see you for another twelve days. It's going to kill me.

CATE
Not gonna lie, I'm struggling. It's like everything gone wrong so quickly. Can't believe it's so quiet in the city. Can't believe I'm stuck here.

TOM
I'll be out of quarantine soon, then we can be together. Sorry I went away, I had no idea it'd get so bad so quick ... You know.

CATE
Well how could you, it wasn't obvious by that point ...

TOM
Thanks. Though I still feel like a fool. And now we're both alone.

CATE
No we're not, we're speaking now.

She touches the screen with her hand.

CATE
But it's not the same I know, babe.

TOM
Just wish I could hold you right now. Touch your skin ... Kiss you.

CATE
You'll turn me on Tom, even if it doesn't feel like now's the right time for having fun.

Your Courage, Your Cheerfulness, Your Resolution

TOM

Yeah we've got to carry on though, this could last a long time. Well that's what that Chief Medical Advisor said.

CATE

Don't say it. I can't cope with the idea this is going to last more than a few weeks. I've got my anxiety just about under control, then this ... This happens. If it goes on, then I don't know what I'll do.

TOM

Come on, babe, you've got this.

CATE

Stop it, Tom, it's serious. Anyway I hate it when people say that sort of stuff. It's so ... American. When did we all become American?

TOM

I'm just trying to be ...

CATE

Oh, sorry, I didn't mean to snap.

She starts to cry. She puts her head into her hands and looks away from the screen.

CATE

Oh God. I didn't mean to be like that, like a fucking crying little girl. I'm not a little girl. Damn, I'm sorry ... It's just I'm trapped in here. It's like I'm in a prison, I'm so high up I have to use the lift, and last time. You know I told you about last time. When that guy got in. He was ill. He could have killed me with it. Didn't even have a tissue on him. The virus was everywhere. I know it. I just can't face that lift, it's not safe ... I'm trapped here.

Unlocked

Sobs.

> I can't get out. I can't even open a window. And the aircon vent. I've tried taping it up, but I'm sure it's coming through the vent. My asthma. I'm so scared Tom. I don't want to get it.

> TOM
> Come on, we've talked about this. You're young, I know what happened. But that was before, it wasn't you ... You're strong, you'll be all right.

> CATE
> But what if I'm not all right. I'm alone Tom. I'm alone but yet I can tell you I'm alone. I just want someone to hold me Tom. Tell me it's okay and hold me.

Sobbing again.

> God damn it. Stop crying Cate!

She screams in exasperation.

> TOM
> I know. Stay calm. You've got your inhaler, it's going to be okay. Look at me ... Come on look at me ... Yes that better, you know I'll be there as soon as I can. I'd come now but I can't risk it, you know I've been exposed but I'll know soon.

> CATE
> I don't know if I can last that long, Tom, I'm so scared. I don't want it to get me when I'm alone. Who's going to be there for me if I'm ill? What am I going to do, Tom? Eating the same food day after day, as well it's going to make me ill. Then I'll be more ...

Your Courage, Your Cheerfulness, Your Resolution

The screen beeps loudly. A message states, "Unknown participant is waiting to join the call".

TOM
Did you see that?

CATE
Yes.

TOM
I thought this was just the two of us?

CATE
It's supposed to be. I'm only just getting used to this software, maybe it's an error.

TOM
Shall I let them into the call? Maybe it's your mother.

CATE
She doesn't know how to use this stuff. It can't be. Well I don't think so. Perhaps the phone isn't working. Do you think she's okay, I mean she's old ... I haven't spoken today ... Hope she's good, maybe I better check ... Hold on Tom.

CHARACTER #3: ANON joins the call as another window on the computer screen. The figure is greyed out but a silhouette can be seen, probably an adult male.

TOM
Hey. Who's there? You've not got a name it just says Anon on the screen. Is that Sally?

CATE
Mum? Sally is that you? Are you okay? Who is it? Can you hear us?

Unlocked

ANON

Hi. Can you hear me? It's George here. George Thompson, is everything all right there?

CATE

George? Who are you, George? Why are you on the call? Do you know my mum or something? Is everything okay? God please tell me everything is okay?

ANON

Listen to me, I've been told to make a call using this new-fangled device. Sorry if I'm not clear, first time I've used this thing. I hope you can hear me loud and clear?

TOM

Yes. But who are you?

ANON

I want to make sure everyone is all right, that's why I'm on this radio thing to tell you all.

CATE

Er, what do you mean, I don't get this, and how are you on the call?

ANON

I'm just telling everyone what they need to do. To stay well. This enemy isn't going to get us. We're strong, our city. Our country, we're going to beat this enemy. But you've got to stay indoors, don't get hurt, not worth it. Have you got tinned food? Enough for you all?

CATE

Yes, er, I've got food.

Your Courage, Your Cheerfulness, Your Resolution

TOM
Just about, got more pasta than a Sicilian wholesaler ...

ANON
I think I checked everyone has got food. So that's good. Just stay indoors and watch out. I hope you're warm, and the heating working still. If so you can stay in.

CATE
The heating is on. What? Is it going to break, I mean it's April, but will it break?

ANON
We checked everyone had enough fuel to last, I think you'll be warm. Don't go out looking for stuff because you might get it. No good then, if one of us gets it, then it's more likely the whole street will come down. That's no good. Happened down the road. You know about it. So let's bunker down.

CATE
I'm not going to give it to anyone, I'd never do that. That's why I'm not seeing mum ... Did you say you know mum?

ANON
Yes don't go popping round to see the relatives, it'll cause trouble. More danger that way.

CATE
I won't.

TOM
You didn't say who you were?

Unlocked

ANON

We're going to beat this. You know that? The country is going to beat it. We're going to beat it together? You all should know that ...

TOM

Yes. I can tell you're positive. You sound a little crazy but I think it's rubbing off.

ANON

Don't worry about being in your bunker alone. That's how we avoid trouble, I know it's hard. A bit of wartime spirit guys and girls and we'll pull through. As long as you've got your food and you're warm we'll be back to normal and our way to winning.

TOM

Winning?

ANON

Winning the War. We're going to win and one day we'll be having a beer in the park, laughing and singing. Mark my words everyone. We'll win this war.

CATE

I don't know who you are but I like your positivity, you've got good karma.

ANON

So I'm going to finish off by saying I know times are hard for our area but I'm here for you. We're all here for you and when it's over we'll win this war.

TOM

Yes, I think we will.

Your Courage, Your Cheerfulness, Your Resolution

ANON

We'll beat them. We'll beat Jerry and it'll all be good very, very soon. So stay safe. And remember YOUR COURAGE, YOUR CHEERFULNESS, YOUR RESOLUTION, WILL BRING US VICTORY.

TOM

Hold on! Did you just say Jerry? Who are you? I said who are you? Can you actually hear me … ?

CATE

Yes wait, are you … Do you think you're in the War? It's a virus. Yes I know we're going to beat it, but are you …

ANON leaves the call.

TOM

Wow. What was that? I thought he could hear us, I'm not sure … He just kept saying he wanted us safe indoors, and we'd be all right.

CATE

Tom … Look. I'll call you back. I'm sure he said his name was George Thompson. I thought it was a relative of my mum's that why I didn't … Wait a minute, Sally's granddad was called George. I never met him, he died years before I was born.

TOM

What?

CATE

That was her granddad. You don't think? He died in the War. He was a Military Policeman I think. But …

Unlocked

TOM
Don't be crazy. How could ...

CATE
But the War. He was talking about the War. He wanted us to stay safe? He said we'll be okay if we just stayed indoors for a while. My head. It just couldn't be could it? Tom, I'll have to call you back.

CATE clicks terminate on the call. She turns the smart speaker back on and the radio podcast carries on in the background, as she goes back over to the window.

SMART SPEAKER
The planet is just over forty light years away, LHS1140b is unusual in that we've got an unobstructed view of the rocky world. So if radio waves were beamed there and back it'd take double that time for the signal to come back again and reach us, meaning that if you had a call you'd have to have started it in 1940 ...

THE END